Manage the Mess of Family Stress

Gospel Solutions for Everyday Life

RICHARD C. BROWN, PhD

Liguori
LIGUORI, MISSOURI

Imprimi Potest: Harry Grile, CSsR
Provincial, Denver Province, The Redemptorists

Published by Liguori Publications
Liguori, Missouri 63057
To order, call 800-325-9521
www.liguori.org

Library of Congress Cataloging-in-Publication Data

Brown, Richard C., 1935-
 Manage the mess of family stress : Gospel solutions for everyday life / Richard C. Brown.
   p. cm.
 ISBN 978-0-7648-1983-4
 1. Families—Religious life. 2. Christian life—Catholic authors. 3. Stress management. I.
Title. II. Title: Gospel solutions for everyday life.
 BX2351.B76 2011
 248.8'45088282--dc22

                                                                         2010048630

Liguori Publications, a nonprofit corporation, is an apostolate of the Redemptorists. To learn more about the Redemptorists, visit Redemptorists.com

Printed in the United States of America
15 14 13 12 11   5 4 3 2 1
First Edition

Table of Contents

Foreword

Manage the Mess of Family Stress is a valuable book written to help people navigate marriage and family life. Among the greatest concerns I have as a bishop in the Church today are the difficulties that people experience in marriage and family life. Healthy marriages and strong families are the most important institutions in our society and Church. We know that traditional marriage often is under attack in our secular society. Bishops in the United States have started a significant project on marriage and the family, and it is expected that the pastoral letter on this subject will bear much fruit. This book dovetails nicely with that effort.

Dr. Richard Brown makes a fine contribution to wholesome marriage and family life in this book. He draws upon the life of Jesus as shown in the New Testament. He suggests four elements of the behavior of Jesus to help families deal with conflict and stress in today's society—loving servanthood, loving forgiveness, use of intelligence, and speaking out on issues.

As the author points out, these four behaviors are tools that can help married couples deal with stress and conflict in their relationships. The behaviors that Jesus modeled also provide a practical spirituality that can help cultivate spiritual growth and productive peace in one's own family and work life.

In addition, the book provides helpful exercises that family members can use to deal with conflict and stress that crop up in daily life. This book draws from the teachings of Jesus and provides a road map that families can use to develop greater love, self-respect, and peace. I highly recommend it!

—*Most Reverend Michael J. Sheehan,*
Archbishop of Santa Fe, New Mexico

Introduction

Catholics today are searching for ways to handle the stress and conflict of daily life. We desire the confidence that comes from understanding the causes of stress, and we find hope in powerful solutions. We need a workable spirituality—a style of Christlike, practical behaviors that intelligently solve our major concerns and strengthen our follow-through. We also need this workable spirituality so that we can model and teach it to our children. For the non-Mass-attending Catholic, we offer the promise of a confident and hope-filled daily life—one that draws its greatest source of power from the light- and strength-producing Mass.

Bringing this spirituality to parishioners and non-parishioners alike requires concerted effort and input—especially from practicing Catholics like parishioners and parish and diocesan staff members. After reading this book, you will be able to incorporate the wisdom and practices into your daily life. You also will be able to use these tools to evangelize non-practicing Catholic relatives, friends, and others you encounter. The intent is to grow in one's own loving spiritual relationship with God, and also to convince others to join you in that same growth process.

A workable spirituality simply requires four behaviors that Jesus practiced—forgiveness, intelligence, servanthood, and speaking out. We apply these behaviors to four major areas in our lives—family, self, the sacred, and society. Applying these four behaviors that Jesus practiced to these areas helps build a spirituality that works in everyday life for twenty-first-century Catholics.

I now bring to you—whether you are a current or former parishioner of the Catholic Church—these four behaviors that have proven to powerfully assist in dealing with life's stresses and conflicts. Practicing these behaviors—forgiveness, intelligence, servanthood, and speaking out—provides the logic and strength that counteract various causes of conflict and stress. Through our own Christlike behaviors—along with help from God's light and strength—we are capable of resolving difficulties and complications in our daily lives.

Based upon four Christlike behaviors, this spirituality provides a common-sense and psychologically sound solution when you encounter stress and conflict. Learning to approach life with this consistent behavior pattern allows you to accomplish what you need to do on a daily basis with confidence, hope, and peace. By practicing these behaviors, you can find lasting resolutions to problems and issues that create stress and conflict in your life. By putting these behaviors into practice, your short- and long-term emotional health also will flourish. Doing the exercises in this book will provide you with quick results.

Behaviors covered in this book help people in all walks of life. Whether you are married or single, a parent or grandparent, a lay person or a religious, this book has some solutions and tools for you. Children also can benefit from the concepts outlined in this book as adults learn, teach, and practice the spiritual behaviors in their daily lives. The book also teaches you how to apply this spirituality in the workplace and in other areas of daily life. My own personal experience comes from ten years of monastic life as a teaching brother, and later as a spouse, parent, grandparent, teacher, and counselor.

We need greater wisdom and strength to deal with challenges every day. This need comes from the sacred connections that are necessary and central to human existence. Made in God's image and likeness, and possessing intellect and will, our purpose is to develop an eternal love relationship with God and each other. God grants us the wisdom to help our intellect search for truth in the various decisions and situations we encounter daily. God also supplies us with the strength we need so that we can follow through on the wisdom we discover while working through our problems. The greatest source of this help comes from attending Sunday and weekday Mass. "Give us each day our daily bread" (Luke 11:3).

Many Catholics, however, do not attend weekly Mass. One of the greatest human mysteries may be the insanity of choosing not to tap into the power of weekly Mass. By participating in weekly Mass, we can receive help and practical solutions for solving a multitude of problems and issues we encounter every day.

Once you experience the power of Jesus' behaviors, how they can help you deal with stress and conflict, and how they can bring you peace, you are then better able to model these behaviors for the children in your life. They will observe the beauty and power in your approach to life. By observing your Christlike behavior, they will be receptive to what you have to say. In the end, they may choose to experience for themselves this stable way of life—one that centers on a loving relationship with God, with others, and with themselves as they tune in to their own legitimate needs.

May Jesus' behaviors—along with the grace promised in the sacramental life of the Church—take you deeper into the rich and fruitful daily life that God's love has always intended for you. Confidence and hope can be yours through this spirituality. It is a spirituality that works. It helps today's Catholic meet the challenges encountered in daily life, and it will help you in yours.

Chapter One

Does God Want Stress and Conflict in Our Daily Lives?

I began a discussion among a group of families at my parish with the following question: "Who makes this beautiful universe we see at night, and the fruit trees we see during the day?" A nine-year-old immediately responded, "Jesus does!" That extraordinary wisdom went to the heart of all that God's love does for us. God created the universe, God makes our daily bread, God is one of us...all is God's love for us.

This leads us to the central question in this chapter: Does God want stress and conflict in our daily lives? Who among us ever wants stress and conflict for a loved one? No one, of course. So why do we experience stress and conflict in our own lives? The answer is, we do it to each other and to ourselves. Even God in Jesus suffered stress and conflict as a human. Fortunately, Jesus left us with some logical, practical examples of how to cope. This book is designed to help us apply his sound wisdom in our daily lives.

When I was a sophomore in high school, I decided to break a long-distance hiking record with two of my buddies. That June, we would trek from the Phoenix Desert into the north country, full of Arizona's forests and streams. Once they found out about my goal, my mom and dad looked at me and said, "You want to cross the desert in the summer? What about the rattlesnakes? No way, Richard!"

I persisted, and in the end, they gave me reluctant permission to go on the hike. As it turned out, we broke the record—even though one of my friends ended up in the hospital with bloodied feet. My parents were right about the rattlesnakes. We survived five separate encounters.

I wanted to be in charge of my own life. I wanted to rely on my own decisions. My parents' judgment was more sound than mine, but fortunately, they took the risk of allowing me to have this experience where I had to trust myself and my own decisions. The thrill of adventure remains with me to this day. My desert experience taught me to trust my own God-given intelligence. Rewind to that pre-hike confrontation. Both my parents and I wanted to be in charge of the situation. This, of course, created stress and conflict.

The stress of dealing with different personalities—whether found in the family or at work—begins when one leaves the womb. We are like snowflakes, and no one is identical to the other. God gives each of us a unique combination of skills. The shadow side of that gift is that those very differences—our God-given personalities, talents, and skills—also tend to create the most conflict and stress in our relationships. Understanding this dynamic will allow us to pour the concrete foundation on which we can build the confidence, hope, peace, and joy that God wants for us. We also will address emotional illness and sin, which are less common but can create conflict and stress.

What Is Stress?

Who does not experience stress each day? Your children resist what you cooked for breakfast. Traffic is worse than usual. A client misses your lunch appointment. Your teen misses the 10 o'clock curfew. If you stop and pay attention to your physical or mental state, you can feel the tangible symptoms of stress—tight neck muscles, dry mouth, and a feeling of fatigue or depression. These are signs that your nervous system is responding to protect you from danger—whether physical, emotional, or mental. Wanting to protect you from danger, God created these reactions in you.

Stress tells you that all is not well, and that you need to act to reduce or eliminate the stress. You may experience stress as you begin backing out of an icy driveway. Or perhaps you will feel stressed on your way to a family party where you know a certain relative will throw a negative comment in your direction. Your body automatically prepares to handle the danger, and as it does, you experience stress.

We also can experience stress when problems arise and solutions are needed. "Should I tell this new potential mate about my feelings of love?" "What should I do about my serious job dissatisfaction?" "What should I do about my unruly teen?" "How can we get our budget under control?" Stress can cause anxiety, worry, sleeplessness, sadness, and fear.

One Quick Remedy

I have used a rose petal as a simple tool to help hundreds of seminar participants across the United States relieve their feelings of stress. Facing many problems in their ministries, these church leaders are first asked to think of a problem that is bothering them the most. They are then asked to take one rose petal and use all five senses to experience it. They notice the beauty of its color and design. They feel the softness. They rustle it next to their ear. They smell and taste this physical beauty God made. When I ask who still has that stressful problem in their mind, usually only one or two people raise their hands. Why?

God has given us a psychological gift. Our system can concentrate on only one thing at a time. So when we experience stress, concentrating on any physical object with our five senses does the trick—at least for the moment. We may need to repeat the exercise a few minutes later, but with each repetition we are building our system's awareness that we can control our stress and reduce its mental and physical symptoms. We can take charge and control our stress.

The Primary Causes of Conflict

Having learned a simple way to reduce stress, its underlying causes still require remedies. So we need to take a closer look at natural personality differences. The potential for even daily conflict automatically arises whenever two or more people relate with each other. Because we each have different skills and talents as part of our unique, God-given personalities, we have different needs. As a result, we may enjoy different things than others.

You may be skilled when it comes to taking charge and enjoy being a decision-maker. Someone else may enjoy and be skilled in acting independently, preferring not to make decisions for others. Another person may be more dependent, wanting someone else to make decisions and take charge. All three people have different abilities and skill levels, and as a result, they each have different preferences when it comes to making decisions and taking the lead in decision-making.

Behaviors of Jesus That Naturally Eliminate Conflict and Stress

Most helpful in handling conflict and stress in daily life are four behaviors that Jesus modeled: servanthood, forgiveness, the use of the intellect, and speaking out.

Servanthood means to love one another and ourselves as God loves us. Asked to summarize what his teachings were all about, Jesus replied: "You shall love the Lord your God with all your heart, and with all your soul, and with all your mind." This is the greatest and the first commandment. Another similar commandment is: "You shall love your neighbor as yourself" (Matthew 22:39). We see Jesus' own loving servanthood in the way he behaved during the time he spent with us on earth. Concern for and acting on the needs of a loved one demonstrate the behavior of love.

Jesus takes care of the needs of a wedding party that, to the chagrin of the bride and groom, runs out of wine. He feeds five thousand men, and most likely, their families. He lovingly converts a Samaritan woman who has been divorced five times, and then turns her into his first missionary of God's love for her entire town. Jesus serves his

Father and us throughout his suffering and death on the cross. Jesus makes the Eucharist available for our embrace every day throughout the world. The same God who gives us love and invites us to respond to the needs of others as well as our own also brings peace that erases conflict and stress.

The *forgiveness* Jesus modeled and talked about provides another behavior that directly counters conflict and stress. We face harm from someone in the course of each day—whether through a verbal put-down, forgetfulness, ignorance of our needs, a disdainful look, flagrant lack of cooperation, lies, and countless other ways. People do not always meet our needs in a loving way—whether intentionally or unintentionally. Our responsibility in these situations lies in returning the harm done to us by restoring the presence of love.

Like the father of the prodigal son in Jesus' parable (Luke 15:11–32), our response to harm should be a response of love. We find a way to "throw a party" for those who have harmed us. We listen and respond to their needs. From a behavioral standpoint, forgiveness works in a practical way by building up the relationship of love that another person has broken by harming us. How can conflict and stress continue in the face of the loving behavior of forgiveness? It cannot. But if the harm continues, Jesus gives us full permission to stop the harm, honoring our right to be loved.

This brings us to a third behavior of Jesus—*the use of our intellect*, which can logically and psychologically counteract conflict and stress. When we practice forgiveness as described above, we may need to balance the love we have for the person who has harmed us with the recognition that we have a right to walk away from the negative behavior. Our intellect—our power to arrive at truth in solving life's situations—needs to come into play when we are called to achieve this kind of balance in our interactions with others.

The most effective use of intellect in conflict resolution is to ask questions, which forces the intellect to engage in problem-solving. I ask parents and church leaders in my seminars to take an unsolved problem and bombard it with one question after another. Nearly everyone reports the discovery of a new direction, as well as a possible workable solution or decision.

In applying the intellect to a situation that requires forgiveness, we can find balance by asking three questions: 1) How can I behave in a loving way in response to behavior that has harmed me? 2) What are my legitimate needs in this situation? 3) How might I meet the needs in both (1) and (2)—preferably at the same time?

For example, I may discover that someone in the workplace has told a lie about me, or revealed a truth about me that threatens my reputation or standing among fellow workers. I may conclude that the person chose to engage in the behavior for his or her own benefit. So I respond with a friendly gesture and ask that person to lunch. Over lunch, I mention hearing that someone had hurt my reputation at work. I might ask: "What would you suggest I do to correct that?" Creative thinking like this results from asking questions. If you continue to ask yourself questions in problem situations, you will increasingly experience the power of your God-given intellect. It is there to help you deal with all of life's difficulties. Over time, you will learn to trust your judgment.

The fourth behavior of Jesus that naturally helps resist and conquer conflict and stress is *speaking out*. Even if we are trying to listen to and respond to the needs of others, and even if we are practicing loving forgiveness for harms done, we still may not make headway in dealing with the conflict and stress that comes from our relationships. So we must use this final behavior of speaking out in defense of our own needs and the needs of others.

In Jesus' life, one of the most striking examples of this behavior took place in the Temple when he spoke out about the behaviors of the Jewish leaders, the Pharisees, and the pastors of individual synagogues. In Matthew 23—the week before his crucifixion—Jesus challenged them and their behavior. He called them "hypocrites" seven times, "blind fools" four times, "whitened sepulchers with dead men's bones inside," and many other names to admonish them about their tarnished behavior as religious leaders. Jesus was clearly in conflict with them. And despite Jesus' other attempts to defuse the conflict, they decided to put him to death. Jesus tried to crack their rigid mind-set and resolve the conflict by speaking out—or as some would say, by calling a spade a spade.

These behaviors of Jesus logically and psychologically make sense as ways to deal with conflict and stress. Though Jesus has many other behaviors for us to model, these four taken together provide an ideal package for dealing with daily life at home and work. If the primary cause of conflict is a difference in personalities, servanthood will be an effective antidote because it perceives and responds to others' needs and differences. The harm caused by others' personality differences—as well as from any emotional illness or outright sin—is countered by our forgiveness.

In the first two solutions of servanthood and forgiveness, the use of intellect to balance others' needs against our own legitimate needs requires rational judgment and sound problem-solving. This results from asking questions that get at what makes sense.

When the first three solutions fail to resolve conflict and stress, we can speak out so that our needs or the needs of others are responded to. Speaking out allows others to hear and respond to our needs, and also to forgive us or ask for our forgiveness when the ideal relationship of love needs to be restored. God wants this love for the sake of a peaceful and fruitful life for us all.

The Mass: Source of Strength to Practice the Solutions

Jesus not only models wise behaviors, he provides the strength to practice them. Every word of the Mass—including each word in the daily Scripture readings—shouts out the basic lessons of what our human existence is all about. For example, we say and hear petitions for help from the three persons of God, and from Mary and the other saints. We ask forgiveness. We hear of peace. We praise God, the almighty maker of our "daily bread." We offer our lives to this God. We receive God into ourselves for intimate conversation.

All the while in the Mass, our Catholic theology supports that we are in the midst of the greatest outpouring of grace available to mankind—that is, God's light and strength. By our simple, conscious, loving participation in the words and actions of the Mass, our daily need for answers and strength is filled up—much like that fountain of living water. "The water that I will give will become in them a spring of water gushing up to eternal life...God is spirit, and those who worship him must worship in spirit and truth" (John 4:14; 24). Our spirit's primary powers are intellect and will, with the former giving us the light of truth and sound judgment, and the latter the strength to follow through on that truth. Jesus' presence in the Mass brings us this power of God to deal with the problems of our own unique life journey. Later, we will explore specific behaviors at Mass that can enhance our openness to the graces that address specific needs in our family and work lives.

An Exercise of Love and Grace for the Whole Family

The strength and inspiration I needed to produce this entire book came from experiencing the excitement of family members of all ages who engaged in the following exercise. For a couple of years, I had used this exercise with diocesan and parochial Catholic leaders throughout the United States. They encouraged me to bring this message to their parishioners. I now have done that—thanks to the insightful, grace-filled help of my own parish's catechetical leader. Two experiments—one with her families in RCIC groups, and the other in her Family Faith groups—convinced me to write this book and provide readers with exercises and supportive, practical applications. What follows is a process that parents, grandparents, relatives, and friends can put into practice.

Gather the family together at the dining table. Place them in a circle in pairs, with at least one older child paired with children who are younger than six or seven. (Parents will practice this with each other in Chapter Two on marriage.) You can add ten to twelve other friends or relatives.

The first person to speak in each pair describes to his partner a need he has at that time. "I need help on a school assignment I have to do." "I need help figuring out what to fix for dinner tonight." "The new puppy won't leave me alone."

The second person in each pair responds to the need of her partner, offering advice or stating how she will help out. "I will give you an hour's help on your assignment." "Hot dogs? I will be glad to cook them and warm the buns." "The puppy likes you the best. But call me when you want a break."

Then have the second person state a need, and the first person offer help or advice in response.

Mom or Dad then says, "We have just practiced servanthood—being a servant to each other out of our love for each other. God gives us our life, our food, the clouds and sunsets, trees and materials to build our house, and gives us each other. Everything serves us because God loves us. He wants us to always listen to what others need and do what we can to help because we love each other. That is what family and eternity is all about—our love relationships with each other and God, as opposed to conflict and stress."

Chapter Two

Marriage Solutions for Stress and Conflict

John and Mary had both graduated from Saint Mary's College of California. They met while working for the same software company in Phoenix. Sitting together in the company lunchroom after work, they had started a conversation that would continue for hours on their first date later that week. They enjoyed spending time with each other, soon fell in love, and decided to get married.

I counseled and tested more than seven hundred "we're in love" couples at the Franciscan Renewal Center in Paradise Valley, Arizona. Based on researched psychological causes of divorce, I could see that more than half of these young lovers had relationships that could end up in divorce. The couples in this group had significant differences in personality—especially in areas like decision-making, socializing preferences, and how open they were with their feelings.

In American culture—as in many others—people tend to believe that if you fall in love, you should get married. Yet—to give God a break in the face of such potential irrationality—each of us is given an intellect with which to reason out life's decisions. If potential marriage partners would only listen to the answers they received by asking themselves intelligent questions, perhaps some of them would say to themselves: "Yes, I'm in love, but I don't think I can handle this relationship for a lifetime."

Control issues were the most common cause of male-female conflict in this group, along with differing needs related to socializing and sharing feelings. Yet, as I discovered with those seven hundred couples, it can take only *one* personality skill similarity—such as both liking to socialize—to lead some in-love couples to the conclusion that, "This is the only one for me," or, "This will last forever."

If potential couples made the better choice of seeking a more broadly compatible relationship, the divorce rate would drastically decline due to less relationship conflict and stress. Diocesan premarital testing can be a major stumbling block when the questions focus on how much agreement exists on the informational sides of marriage. A test that concentrates on questions about whether the couple agrees on financial issues, or the household tasks that each person will handle does little to expose deeper personality differences that often result in divorce. This testing method also fails to help couples learn how to teach their children about choosing compatible marriage partners.

Factors of Marriage Compatibility

We saw in the previous chapter how personality differences can create conflict. Now we also see how falling in love can sometimes override rational thinking when it comes to choosing a life partner. Choosing well is difficult. So where can we find hope for a long-lasting, peaceful, enriching marriage for those who may have made a less-than-excellent choice? If you toss up a hundred coins—one at a time—the odds of getting about half tails and half heads is normal and represents pure chance. Similarly, the fifty percent divorce rate may reflect how an uneducated choice—combined with a falling-in-love dynamic—can produce the same pure chance results.

How do we make an educated choice? The primary causes of divorce reside in natural personality differences. First, we need to explore our own unique personality skills and traits. We then need to understand how those skills and traits create enjoyment when they are similar to our partner's, and how personality traits and skills can generate conflict and stress when they are opposite or different than ours.

I began this study of human personality skills more than thirty years ago in my doctorate dissertation research. My research explores the sources of stress between high school students and their teachers. I have found that Edwin Megargee's research, as well as a 460-item questionnaire—the California Psychological Inventory—provide the most accurate assessment of human personality skills. Based on those insights, what follows is the result of my efforts throughout my years of counseling others. My goal was to create a simple self-assessment of what appear to be the most useful skills, as well as information about how those skills and traits can produce interpersonal enjoyment or conflict.

The following skills or traits indicate what to look for as you evaluate your own personality, as well as the personality skills and traits of others who you encounter at home, work, and elsewhere. The examples provided show how conflict can arise in relation to each skill or trait.

Evaluate yourself as strong (S), medium (M), or low (L) in these twelve skills:

1. Decision-making

I trust my own judgment and try to convince others to follow it. I am a natural leader. I value my own opinion. I like to take charge. I do not enjoy other people contradicting my judgment.

Example: John is in love and decides he wants to marry Susan. Susan—while also in love—decides they try to control each other too much. As a result, Susan concludes that she should not marry John.

                                            Circle one: S M L

2. Sociability

I enjoy group situations. I like small talk. I do not enjoy unsociable people who will not return my small talk efforts. I feel energized when I go into a group or family setting, such as an Easter dinner.

Example: Three-year-old Jennifer is a non-stop talker. Dad gets irritated and leaves the room, saying he needs some "alone time."

Circle one: S   M   L

3. Organization

Whether at work or at home, I like to have everything in its proper place. I like order in how I do things. At times I listen to others' needs to the detriment of my own legitimate needs.

Example: Mary gets irritated at the messiness of her child and spouse who show little or no concern about the effects of their behavior on her or others.

Circle one: S   M   L

4. Responsibility

When I have a task to do, I get it done on time. I believe in attention to duty, and I discipline myself. I avoid addictive behaviors or habits.

Example: At his weekly office meeting, Harry gets irritated when fellow employees admit they have not finished a task that needs to be completed so others can effectively complete their work.

Circle one: S   M   L

5. Logical intelligence

Generally, I prefer to solve problems using step-by-step logic, rather than settling for quick answers. Math was one of my favorite subjects in school.

Example: Alice gets angry with her husband and teenager when, on important matters, they make snap decisions or decisions that they have not thought out in a logical manner.

Circle one: S   M   L

6. Intuitive intelligence

I am an original thinker who can think outside the box. Creative intuition allows me to arrive at the truth quickly when I am problem-solving. My spouse and friends sometimes are startled by the speed at which I arrive at my decisions.

Example: David feels irritation at the slow, step-by-step way his boss must think through how to resolve a new office problem.

Circle one: S M L

7. Artistic intelligence

I enjoy beauty in one or more of its many physical forms—music, art, drama, dance, as well as in the natural beauty of the outdoors or in the human form. I like to create beauty through one or more artistic pursuits.

Example: As a child, grandmother Anne's parents ridiculed her interest in playing a neighbor's violin. As a result, she never pursued any musical interests in her early years. In her seventies, she decided to buy a cheap violin so she could finally learn how to play.

Circle one: S M L

8. Counseling

I can tell how people are feeling even when they do not articulate their thoughts or feelings. People feel comfortable sharing their feelings or concerns with me, and they appreciate my insights regarding their feelings.

Example: Though still in his teens, Mark already is aware that his friends seek him out to talk out their problems. He enjoys being able to help them. He has difficulty with his father, who does not seem to understand or have any interest in Mark's feelings.

Circle one: S M L

9. Nurturance

Taking care of the physical needs of others is a joy for me—whether through cooking, volunteering at Saint Vincent de Paul to help the poor, or showing kindness toward the homeless.

Example: Barbara enjoyed cooking a meal for her friend, Dennis. But he could not understand her intense interest in spending so much time preparing the food.

Circle one: S M L

10. Flexibility

I judge new situations and people I meet on their own merits. I do not have a negative or narrow outlook on life, and I do not carry judgments like: "Most men are bad" or "Teens are always a problem."

Example: As a single mom, Mary enjoys how she is able to be flexible in dealing with each new situation in raising her children. She gets upset with her own mother, who insists that every child should be punished for misbehavior rather than first asking why they engaged in the behavior in the first place and then deciding what to do in response.

Circle one: S   M   L

11. Tolerance

I enjoy all types of people, regardless of differences in race, religion, or personality. I am uncomfortable with people who fear or pass judgment on those who are different from them.

Example: Scott joined a protest march with one hundred thousand people—a group that was mostly Hispanic. He later was upset when he received a negative response from his church friends after telling them he saw a biblical quote—"Treat strangers in your midst as brothers and sisters"—on one of the signs.

Circle one: S   M   L

12. Emotional health

I do not feel anxiety. I do not irrationally attack others in anger or put them down. I am at peace. I reach out in loving service to others. I am attentive to my own legitimate needs.

Example: As a pastor, Father John is comfortable dealing with daily problems he encounters while managing his parish. He has concern for a fellow pastor at another parish who constantly worries about problems and who routinely experiences difficulty in falling asleep.

Circle one: S   M   L

How the Twelve Personality Skills Cause Conflict

The greatest source of conflict and stress as people interact with one another comes from the act of decision-making. This skill, and how it can create conflict, is complicated but critical to our understanding of interpersonal conflict. The other eleven skills can create conflict and stress when a person possesses more or less of that skill than another person.

Control is the issue that comes up most often when people discuss interpersonal conflict related to decision-making. "You are trying to control me" often is a statement heard in home situations. At work we may hear, "He is such a micro-manager." Both comments reflect irritation or anger directed at someone who likes to take charge, and who often is skilled in decision-making.

The two types of people who *dislike* control from others generally are people who are either independent or want to be the in-charge person themselves. The fully independent person does not want to be controlled and does not want to control others.

Even two non-controlling personalities who prefer depending on others' decision-making, can sometimes experience conflict when they blame each other for not taking charge in a particular situation.

Control issues cause the majority of home and workplace conflicts. In counseling families, I often found a control issue at the heart of poor school motivation or performance, as well as conflict over how to handle a teen's behavior. With her independent personality, sophomore Lillian often waged open warfare against her dad, a former Marine sergeant who was determined to control her.

John and Jill, a married couple, came to a counseling session red-faced with anger. They had spent the last hour arguing about which screwdriver to use in the repair of their vacuum sweeper. With the rubber belt broken, they needed to remove the bottom plate, which had two large screws. Jill argued for a Phillips screwdriver to deal with the star head of the screw. John insisted on using the flat head of the "original" kind of screwdriver. Either kind would work, obviously.

But two high-control decision-makers wanted their way to prevail in the situation.

A logical way to reduce control conflicts is to give both people an opportunity to be in charge, and to use their talent in the situation. In home and work environments, it is possible to separate areas of responsibility. Let each leader make decisions in their own respective area. Another logical way to lessen conflict is to take turns verbalizing judgments in a calm, logical manner. Each person is in charge for the moment.

The remaining eleven skills or talents can create conflict, depending on an individual's skill level and how his skill level differs from the other person's. You can gauge the differences in skill level by how much people enjoy using a skill or talent. The person who has strong social skills generally enjoys group settings and talking to others. The person with less skill in this area often will complain of having to go to one more party.

Logic suggests resolving conflict by accommodating each person's different enjoyments or needs—which often come from a person's skills or talents. We see this accommodation in Jesus' behavior of loving servanthood—a behavior in which people actively notice and attend to each other's needs.

In conclusion, natural personality differences often provide understanding and insight into what produces conflict and stress in relationships. If your needs are not being met because another person does not share the same personality skills, this can create stress and conflict in that relationship. Anything you can do to meet the other person's needs—or enable him to meet yours—can reduce stress.

Jesus' Behavior Can Reduce Marriage Conflict

The behavior of servanthood that Jesus spoke of and modeled fits this problem of meeting each other's needs. Personality differences can cause conflict because partners sometimes do not meet each other's needs. If a person likes to be in control and be the decision-maker, but is married to an independent spouse who does not like to be controlled, both parties may be unable to meet each other's needs. The behavior of servanthood, as practiced in the exercise at the end of the last chapter, requires us to listen and respond to each other's needs—even when those needs are different from our own.

To humbly deal with my spouse's need to not be controlled makes me uncomfortable and irritated. But this is true spirituality—truly behaving as Jesus did, and as God wants us to behave, in our relationships with others. Despite the suffering it can cause us, we reach out and love our neighbor. In speaking to the Samaritan woman at Jacob's well, Jesus initiated the dialogue by asking her to help him satisfy his physical need for a drink of water. Successful relationships center on meeting each other's needs with acts of love.

The most powerful solution for managing the majority of marital conflicts is found in performing loving acts to address the different needs of each partner. Even so, there are other behaviors and tools that can help resolve conflict within a marriage. Forgiveness, listening to one's own legitimate needs, intelligent balancing of needs, and speaking up for oneself are some of Jesus' other behaviors that can provide needed help as well.

Many Marriages Can Be Saved

Practicing servanthood behavior modeled by Jesus provides hope for saving many more marriages. The primary cause of divorce can be attributed to making the wrong choice in a life partner—in other words, marrying someone who is not naturally compatible. In such a marriage, partners often are unable to meet each other's needs over a lifetime. In such instances, however, servanthood can logically preserve marriages because partners must watch for and respond to each other's needs. For example, both partners may have a strong need to be the decision-maker in the relationship. In such cases, the following may help preserve a marriage:

Each person understands the partner's need to be the primary decision-maker, leader, and the dominant one who is in charge in the relationship.

Both partners routinely ask themselves and each other: "How can I help my partner practice the skill of being in charge?"

The following can be used when both partners have a need to be in charge:

Divide areas of responsibility in the marriage. Areas might include finances, children, chores, and dealing with certain relatives.

Learn to listen to each other's initial judgment on all matters, but leave the final decision to the partner who has that particular area of responsibility.

In summary: The behavior of servanthood enables us to listen to and act on each other's needs—even when doing so makes us uncomfortable, anxious, and even dissatisfied. But the degree of conflict and stress will lessen over time if both partners are able to exercise their need for decision-making and have that leadership respected by the other person.

Regarding the other eleven skills, simply listen to the differing needs of the other person and act on them. In sharing feelings, for example, each partner needs to understand and respect the other person's differences when it comes to sharing feelings. Developing strategies so that both partners can share feelings in a way that is comfortable—"your way," then "my way"—helps lessen conflict.

When partners listen to and act on each other's differing needs, the reduction of conflict and stress provides concrete promise for less buildup of anger and dissatisfaction, which can lessen the likelihood of divorce. Combined with forgiveness, use of the intellect, and speaking out regarding one's needs, the four solutions Jesus modeled can help a couple cultivate grace-filled strength in a peaceful, enriching, and lifetime relationship.

Some marriage incompatibilities will remain unsolvable. The level of strife resulting from personality differences can produce emotional illness that wipes out the quality of life for one or both partners. A diocesan annulment judge was asked at a public meeting: "What percentage of your cases are granted an annulment when they go through all the necessary paperwork?" His answer? Ninety-six percent. Reasonable commitment levels between partners remains an issue, along with the absence of an accurate discernment process when people choose a life partner.

An Exercise for Marriage Partners

To help address each other's needs, marriage partners are encouraged to follow the activity outlined for families at the end of the last chapter. In this exercise, however, there are only two people participating in this loving experiment as marriage partners listen and respond to each other's needs. Setting aside a minimum of ten minutes a day to repeat this exercise is both practical and ideal.

Chapter Three

Parenting Makes God's Love Possible

After school, Dad brings first-grader Marilyn to the family's comics and action figures store. For the moment, Grandpa is pinch-hitting at the store owned by his son. Anderson and his girlfriend Angelica have stopped by with his little girl and her boy—both around Marilyn's age. Marilyn gives Grandpa a hug and hurries to play with the other kids in the "children's section" with its many toys and area rug. Awhile later, Marilyn's mom arrives from her work at a preschool center. She helps her daughter with her homework, and then fixes an evening meal after the store closes. On Sunday after attending Mass, Marilyn and her parents will leave town for a fun day at Grandma and Grandpa's cabin in the woods.

In this brief story we have all the main elements involved in raising today's child. Marilyn has loving care and support from her parents, grandparents, adult friends of her parents and their children, and her school friends. Loving care for a child comes especially from adults, but also from other children. God must regard the raising of children as the most important life task for the majority of adults. So much of emotional health and lifetime productivity rests on parents' child-development skills. The parent is God's primary instrument of love for the dependent, vulnerable child.

An unusual but powerful example of children's loving care and support of each other appeared in a recent Associated Press news item. A mother was pregnant with her seventeenth child. An interviewer asked the father how they dealt with so many children. The father responded, saying that it worked as a result of teaching their children servanthood—the constant loving behavior of sibling attentiveness in recognizing and dealing with each other's needs.

A Parent's Twelve Skills Versus a Child's Twelve Skills

The twelve skills outlined in Chapter Two provide the most important understanding needed by parents when raising and loving their children. "Who is this unique child of mine? How is this child unique and different from me?" A child's strong personality skills create a corresponding need. Loving that child requires meeting those needs—even though we may not possess those same needs ourselves. A sociable child may not share our low need for sociability. But we lovingly listen to them gab, and encourage and support their relationships with other more sociable friends and relatives. This parental servanthood—demonstrated by recognizing and meeting a child's unique needs—is the instrument by which God lovingly meets those needs.

Chapter Two provides an examination of who this unique child is, as well as how she compares to our own uniqueness. Four natural questions help us examine the skills that match:

1. *What are my child's strengths, personality-wise, and what are mine?*

2. *How can I lovingly meet the unique needs that are a result of my child's strengths?*

3. *Which of my child's strengths are likely to irritate me as a result of not possessing those same strengths myself?*

4. *Which of my strengths are likely to irritate my child— particularly if my child does not have the same ones?*

Cultivating this parental understanding of these dynamics in the parent-child relationship provides the necessary wisdom for dealing intelligently with the most common causes of family conflict and stress.

The following are just a few examples of differences that can exist in the parent-child relationship, and also between siblings:

Decision-making: Mom wants her daughter, Jill, to feed the family dog before breakfast. Jill insists on doing it after breakfast.

Socializing: At dinner, Johnny tells his father all about what went on that day at school. Dad concentrates on cutting his rib-eye steak, barely offering an occasional "oh" in response.

Nurturing: Jill loves to fix toast for her twin brother Johnny every morning. She butters his toast lavishly and often chooses the jam. Johnny generally tolerates this gesture but sometimes objects saying, "You are not my mother!"

Use of the Intellect

Meeting the unique personality needs of children—as well as all their other needs—places a tremendous demand on parents' intellect. Jesus relied on his human intellect to deal with the many problems and decisions of his ministry, including others' dependency on his leadership. His apostles left all to follow him. More than likely, Jesus was involved in the many organizational decisions involved in their daily life together. We catch a glimpse of this when Jesus asked, "How many loaves do you have?" (Matthew 15:34) when faced with five thousand hungry listeners.

Jesus' question supplies us with the best example of how to use the intellect in solving parental problems. Since a question forces the intellect to engage, asking questions is the correct first step in dealing with a child's needs. By studying Jesus' example, we see that asking questions about needs, problems, and situations provides us with a great starting point. We gather facts for the intellect, which then can help us identify a solution. We may never have to figure out how to feed a hungry crowd of five thousand. But we may suddenly be confronted with the question of how to feed a group of neighborhood children tagging along behind our sociable and leadership-oriented first-grader, who asks, "What's for lunch, Mom?"

In coming up with workable solutions to address our child's legitimate needs, we may jump from one creative question to another as we gather facts and insights. Jesus and Mary used this approach, often asking questions as a way of finding solutions to problems in their lives. We ask questions because our God-given intellect supplies the truth, and helps us find ways to meet our needs, and find answers to life's problems.

Fun Times

Parents who are wondering how to be an instrument of love to their children can find excellent insight by thinking back to the fun and special times they enjoyed during their own childhood. As I look back on my own childhood, memories that float to the surface include the family car trips where Mom would read to us from an Arizona road map book that described historical events that had taken place along each main road we traveled. Our summer vacations to the Molly Butler forest cabin rentals included catching trout as we meandered up Christopher Creek. Then came the cool rain each afternoon. In the evening, we would watch the tail-slapping beavers push branches across placid dam ponds.

Another summer memory for me is the weeklong visit with our cousins at their cattle ranch. My aunt would make us an angel food cake if we would collect two dozen chicken eggs among the big bales of hay. Years later, I learned that only a dozen eggs were needed for the recipe. So in gathering the eggs for the angel food cake, we had also helped my aunt. These are just a handful of memories from my childhood, but they were all such fun. I loved to solve problems—whether it involved catching a fish or searching for hidden eggs. Looking back on the fun times we've had, we are reminded of how good life can be—despite the stress and conflict that sometimes come our way. Existence itself is fun. And through the insightful, loving, fun-filled care of a parent, children can experience and receive God's love.

God Times for Children

Parents today know the importance of providing newborns with as many experiences as possible—doing so helps the physical brain in its development. Smelling a flower, seeing a butterfly, tasting the first bite of applesauce, hearing Mom and Dad sing a loving lullaby at bedtime—these are all examples of God's loving goodness and how parents help provide children with new experiences. Frequently exposing children to the world's natural and artistic beauty is an easy way to connect them with God's existence and love for them. Some physical objects—like the family Christmas crèche—also provide opportunities to share some Old and New Testament stories that describe God, Jesus, and Mary.

Once children reach the age of six or seven, the parish religious education program can enrich their knowledge and shape their behavior so that they are able to grow in a personal love relationship with God, the center of human existence. Parents also model the importance of attending Mass, the greatest source of grace for daily living. And as one couple discovered, taking a child outside Mass to deal with a behavior problem can easily be turned into a lesson on how one is supposed to behave during Mass. The same couple discovered that two times did the trick for all five of their children. In Chapter Ten, we will return again to this couple's story as we discuss the role that Mass plays in enriching family life.

Sin in Children

What should parents do about a lying three-year-old? A sin is considered serious when the transgression involved is serious, and the person is aware of the sinfulness of the transgression but commits it anyway. So any "sin" before the age of reason does not meet that criteria. The Church does not provide the sacrament of reconciliation or educate children about the sacrament until after first grade.

God provides every individual from birth with sufficient self-interest for personal survival—which allows each person to act as an instrument of God's love to oneself. A parent who asks, "Why is my child lying?" often can find the answer when considering a child's God-given instinct of self-preservation. "They are trying to get what they want," or "they are trying to protect themselves" are the answers that often correspond to the question.

Negative behavior requires parental correction so that children learn proper behavior. Parental involvement also protects children from harm they may experience when siblings or others react to their "bad" behavior, like stealing. All this aside, parents can relax about their own moral culpability when it comes to child-rearing and the reality of human instinct, which sometimes can cause an individual to be too self-interested—even to the point of objective evil.

Forgiveness and Speaking Out

Parents can discover helpful child-rearing lessons by studying how Jesus modeled and taught forgiveness to others. A child who lives on imagination and emotions may sometimes need the discipline of sound reasoning. While recognizing a child's needs, parents also can keep those needs within rational bounds. At other times, children can do or say hurtful, irrational things to their parents. But parents can use those times to model and teach children how to forgive others. An outburst like, "I hate you, Dad," is an opportunity to respond with forgiveness: "I love you, daughter—let's go play with Fido!"

Most of all, we need to keep in mind that the best example of responding with forgiveness is in the positive, let's-throw-a-party response of the father in Jesus' parable of the Prodigal Son (Luke 15:11–32). When our child hurts us, doing what we can to build the loving relationship is the way God wants us to respond in our relationships—here and for all eternity.

The behavior of speaking out also relates to forgiveness. When our children hurt us, we may need to speak out with the same question that Mary asked of her twelve-year-old son: "Son, why have you done this to us?" (Luke 2:48). In asking that question, we may find that our child did not intend to hurt us. In their minds, they may have had what they considered a good reason for their behavior. By asking the question, we give them the opportunity to speak up—not only about their concerns, but also about any hurt they may be experiencing. As the young Jesus said: "Did you not know that I must be in my Father's house?" (Luke 2:49). Practicing the behavior of speaking out not only helps us to forgive, but it also can help address the legitimate, unmet needs of our child. When we understand the rationale behind our child's behavior, we are then able to come to their defense if siblings, adult relatives, neighbors, and others respond in an irrational, negative way as a result of that behavior. At times, we may even have to defend their rights before our spouse. Speaking out requires intelligent, careful judgment that comes from asking questions and identifying facts in a situation.

Sickness and Special Needs

"How can God allow this serious illness to happen to my child?" The stress of a childhood illness can put all of a parent's human and spiritual resources to the test. God does not want illness for our child. We can see that God's grace calls people to become doctors to heal and minister to the sick and injured. The Good Samaritan parable is just one example of God calling all of us to tend to the needs of our neighbor and our children. The natural physical world and other human beings sometimes put us in harm's way. But God gives us the intelligence to avoid or deal with these dangers. Jesus confronted these dangers in his suffering and death on the cross. God the Father did not will that suffering but supported Jesus in dealing with the unavoidable suffering caused by the Pharisee leaders, the weak Pontius Pilate, and the greedy Judas.

God wants loving parents to seek help through prayer when dealing with the sickness and suffering of their children. God is lovingly present and creates good from evil in so many different ways. We can teach our children how to deal with sickness and suffering by modeling prayerful trust and confidence in God.

Some families shoulder burdens related to special-needs children who have serious debilitating conditions like developmental disabilities, physical deformities, and other abnormalities. Despite these hardships, special-needs children and their families are examples of God's special love and concern. Families with special-needs children often experience immediate and long-term stress and conflict. Sometimes parents of special-needs children struggle with the feeling that they are somehow responsible for the condition. In addition, parents of special-needs children often struggle with physical and emotional fatigue. The solution is to take needed time away. Taking time for self-care corresponds with God's loving desire for the parent.

Negative Parental Behavior

In addition to all the positive, loving parental behaviors we have discussed up to this point, we also need to consider the impact that a parent's negative behavior can have on a child. Each of us is made in the image of God and destined for eternal happiness in a loving relationship with God and others. Each individual also has a unique personality. And even though we may sin, we are fundamentally good and worthy. Even so, when we deal with bad behavior, we sometimes allow anger to affect our attitude, feelings, and the way we relate to others. Negative put-downs are never appropriate responses to bad behavior. As parents, we can correct wrong behavior in our children. But in doing so, we must always maintain an overall approach that supports the belief in our child's fundamental worth and goodness. This approach ensures that we keep in mind the truth about who our child is—in spite of any bad behavior on his part.

Personality differences sometimes play a part in a parent's negative responses and reactions. For example, parents who have a high aptitude for decision-making usually have a strong belief in their own judgment. For this reason, parents who are skilled in decision-making need to make sure they do not correct their children's behavior in a negative way. Correcting our children in a negative way can have a lasting impact. Children who experience irrational outbursts sometimes take away the wrong messages from those interactions. They may misinterpret and internalize the message, and as a result, start believing that they are not worthy and that they should not trust their own judgment. Learning how to trust one's own God-given intelligence is a fundamental need on several levels—especially from an emotional and intellectual standpoint. For this reason, children need to be protected from unnecessary negative challenges. They need to learn how to appreciate their own worth and develop confidence in their ability to make sound judgments. Children—especially those between the ages of six and twelve—can learn through self-trust and God's grace that they are able to make good decisions and develop accurate judgments in their relationship with God, others, and themselves.

Parents' Legitimate Interests

The constant demands on parents to provide loving care for the needs of their children also require them to pay attention to and honor their own needs. When parents are aware of their own unique interests and needs, they are better able to accept personality differences in their children. Once again, when parents ask questions like, "How can I cope with my child's constant chatter?" they are able to find sound answers.

Listening to a child's needs and responding to them sometimes can be overwhelming. To avoid the natural buildup of anger and depression that sometimes results from setting personal needs aside, parents also need to take a break from childcare duties to address their own needs for rest and relaxation. In fact, parents need to find respite on a daily basis to do something they enjoy. And finding time weekly—even away from the house—is essential. With help from a relative or trusted babysitter, parents can take time out for dinner with their spouse for a needed break. A weekend getaway also can do wonders—not only for individual restoration, but also as a way to help maintain the marriage relationship.

Practical Applications Summary

✳ A child needs loving attention and care from a wide range of people, including parents, siblings, relatives, and friends of all ages.

✳ Model and teach your child the necessity of listening and responding to the needs of others.

✳ Know and remember your child's unique personality needs so that you are able to meet them. In the process, remember to act on your own unique needs that either match up with or conflict with theirs.

✳ Ask yourself questions as a way of challenging your intellect to discover solutions to problems and ways to meet your child's needs.

✳ Think back to the fun and special times from your own childhood as a way to create fun, worthwhile experiences for your child.

✳ Help your child learn to appreciate God's loving handiwork by constantly pointing out everyday examples like bugs, flowers, and sunsets.

✳ Get your child involved in the parish religious education program to augment your own education efforts at home, and to help him develop more knowledge of and a loving relationship with God.

✳ Make weekly Mass a priority and a major event in your family life so that you can draw needed strength and light to deal with the week's challenges.

✳ Correct your child's bad behavior—like lying or stealing. But in the process, remember that no moral culpability is present before the age of six or seven.

✳ Practice forgiveness, and build the loving relationship you have with your child by reaching out in creative ways.

✳ When necessary, defend your child's legitimate interests and needs—especially when called into question by others.

✻ Teach your child to trust in God's loving presence—even in the midst of sickness and suffering—by modeling the behavior yourself.

✻ When correcting a child's behavior, carefully avoid negative put-downs that can harm her self-worth and cause her to question her own judgment.

✻ Build daily and weekly times into your schedule for doing what you enjoy.

Exercise in Use of the Intellect

Given all the challenges parents face in meeting the constant needs of their children, as well as their own needs and those of their spouse, this seems an appropriate time to discuss the power of the intellect and how to use it to identify solutions to problems. Parents can do this exercise together as a couple, and single parents can do it with a friend or relative. (If doing this exercise with children, simply adapt steps in the exercise to address current challenges in family or school life).

Bring up a current unresolved parenting challenge.

Next, have each participant write a description of the problem, providing as many details as possible.

With eyes closed, have each person bombard the problem with questions as they come to mind. For example, some questions might be: "What other facts are there to consider in this situation?" "What else might be a solution?" "Who else could help solve this issue?" When asking yourself questions, keep an open mind. Stay open to questions that may come from outside-the-box thinking when you ask: "What other questions might I ask myself about this problem?"

Share the thoughts and solutions that occur to you during this process. Most of all, enjoy the process of discovery through the power of your God-given intellect. It can help resolve the daily challenges of child-rearing.

Chapter Four

Helping a Teen Choose

John was ready for college. He knew the major that fit his interests and talents. John would remain in touch with his circle of friends and make new ones. He would choose his future wife carefully, based on a match compatible with the man he knew himself to be. John's confidence in his own unique skills and judgment had sharpened during his teen years, but started in childhood as a result of the observations and support he received from his parents. John knew God personally from reading Scripture, and also through the development of his friendship with Jesus in the Eucharist. By all appearances, John was ready to leave the nest, and well-prepared for the next chapter in his life. If only all teens were as fortunate as John.

God's Wisdom for Raising Teens

After twenty-some years of high school counseling and private-practice family counseling, I stumbled across the succinct wisdom of how to parent teens in the story of Jesus in the Temple. It took Mary and Joseph three days to find their twelve-year-old, after first heading home to Nazareth from Jerusalem. They finally found Jesus still in Jerusalem, sitting among the teachers in the Temple, "listening to them and asking questions. And all who heard him were amazed at his understanding and his answers" (Luke 2:46–47). There in the Temple, Jesus had discovered his skill as a religious teacher. And despite his age, Jesus found himself in a circle of men who already were his peers.

For some time, modern adolescent psychology has identified two tasks that need to be completed from a developmental standpoint during the teen years. During this period, teens need to: 1) discover their unique identity and 2) experience acceptance among their peers. Most parents are very familiar with the latter desire and need that teens have for acceptance. And if they listen carefully enough, parents also are tuned into their teen's struggle to discover their identity through skills and activities they enjoy. This discovery process unfolds as teens learn what they enjoy and are most attracted to in their studies, part-time activities, and through the observation of their parents, relatives, and others. We can see from Jesus' experience that he managed to fulfill both developmental needs during his "escapade" in the Temple. Most parents can appreciate the humor behind the following statement: "He was then 'grounded' for 18 years, until he began his ministry at age 30."

In addition to the valuable lessons observed in the Temple incident, Scripture also provides us with the parable of the Prodigal Son. Mary and Joseph had to forgive Jesus after he disappeared and went to the Temple: "Look, your father and I have been searching for you in great anxiety" (Luke 2:48). But in the parable of the Prodigal Son, Jesus provides parents with additional wisdom for the times when children say or do hurtful things while searching for their unique identities (Luke 15:11–32).

When the prodigal son returned home after having wasted his portion of the family fortune—and perhaps after harming the family name—his father immediately embraced him and threw a party in celebration of his son's homecoming. Through this example, we can see that the father worked to restore the love relationship with his son, rather than first carrying on a dialogue like this: "Are you sorry for what you did? Really sorry? Well, then, I forgive you…" The most powerful act of forgiveness focuses on rebuilding the relationship to restore the love lost by the harm done, rather than holding onto pain. By practicing this loving approach to forgiveness, you can experience immediate, powerful, and grace-filled results. God blesses our attempts to restore love relationships. Doing good for each other and practicing relationship-building forgiveness is what God wants us to do in all our relationships.

The Best Parenting Skills

Teens sometimes challenge their parents by testing their personality differences and skills—particularly when those traits differ from their parents' personality traits. In the process of testing these behaviors, teens may act strange, defiant, and irrational—much like the adolescent Jesus who disappeared for three days.

Once again, we can look to the incident in the Temple and Mary's wisdom in how to deal with teen behavior. Jesus is God, but also fully human—and as such, he exhibited some typical teen behavior. When Mary confronted him about his actions, she first asked: "Child, why have you treated us like this?" (Luke 2:48). The way Mary questioned Jesus' behavior provides an important lesson to parents with teens. In questioning Jesus, she did not berate him. She did not put him down or demean him. She simply asked why he had engaged in the behavior. Mary then told Jesus where she was coming from, and the impact that his actions had on her: "Look, your Father and I have been searching for you in great anxiety" (Luke 2:48).

By asking Jesus why he disappeared for three days, we can see that Mary implicitly accepted the fact that he might have had a legitimate reason for his behavior. Jesus responded: "Why were you searching for me? Did you not know that I must be in my Father's house" (Luke 2:49)? Despite his explanation, Scripture highlights the disconnect between Jesus and his parents when it says, "But they did not understand what he said to them" (Luke 2:50). Even so, Jesus did go back to Nazareth with them where he "increased in wisdom and in years, and in divine and human favor" (Luke 2:52).

In the Temple scene, we see Mary demonstrating good parenting skills. When confronted with our children's seemingly irrational behavior, we need to ask them why they chose to engage in the behavior in the first place. Then we can listen to their rationale. After hearing their explanation, we can determine if they had a good, legitimate reason for behaving the way they did, and we then can provide necessary feedback. If correction needs to be made, we can help them assess what makes sense, what doesn't, and help them arrive at some reasonable solutions and better behaviors for next time.

The following are some practical steps you can follow if you have a teen with natural leadership, take-charge, decision-making skills:

If you and your teen are experiencing conflict, ask her to describe how she sees the situation.

After you understand her point of view, describe how you see the situation.

Even if it feels difficult or uncomfortable, say: "Based on everything we have talked about, I want you to judge what makes the most sense, and what seems to be the most logical approach."

This last step may be the most difficult because, as parents, we risk letting teens make decisions that may be harmful to themselves or others. If this happens, challenge their logic. When challenged, teens often will decide on what seems most rational—especially if they understand that the decision is their final choice among the alternatives you have discussed with them. Sometimes if you have a teen who is a natural leader, he will oppose you—even if you possess the truth about a situation—because he wants to be the decision-maker or the one in charge. By giving him the opportunity to make the final decision, you allow your teen to be the leader in the situation—he has the opportunity to be the one who chooses the most rational response to the situation.

All teens—regardless of whether they are natural leaders—struggle to establish their own unique identity. As a result of this discovery process, they sometimes challenge their parents. The above three-step process often can help resolve conflict in situations where the need to exercise good judgment is a factor. Hopefully you will not need to use the following: "Due to the seriousness of the situation, I as a responsible parent must exercise my right and obligation to make the final decision in this case."

In addition to this three-step process, there are additional tools that parents can use to help teens make some of life's major decisions—like selecting a marriage partner, choosing friends, deciding on a career, and deciding what to do with leisure time.

Helping Teens Prepare for Their Marriage Partner Choice

As parents, we can help our children learn how to make the right decisions. And few decisions are as important as choosing a life partner. What is more important than helping the children we love enrich their lives with the lifetime beauty of marriage, rather than the tragedy, pain, and disappointment of divorce?

During the teen years, children mature and further develop their unique personalities. And as we have observed in Scripture, identifying talents and gifts as Jesus did in the Temple is a critical function of this age. As parents, we often are the first to recognize our children's gifts and talents—sometimes before our children are fully aware of them. But when they reach their teenage years, our children are more self-aware and can more accurately identify who they are in relation to the world around them. This is where parents' awareness and support become so critical. The following is a process that parents can follow to help our children find the right path:

We point out the skills we see in our teens and share our observations with them. After more than twenty years of verifying personality skills based on the testing of hundreds of individuals, I consider the twelve personality skills described in the previous chapter on marriage a solid base from which to draw in making an accurate assessment of our teen's personality and skills. The "S's" are important to note. They can provide the greatest enjoyment in a compatible relationship, and the most dissatisfaction if they differ from our partner's.

We then sit down with our teens when they are in sixth or seventh grade and discuss their existing friendships, evaluating them on the basis of the twelve skills. We ask questions like: "Which friend has skills most similar to yours?" "Which friends irritate you because they lack certain skills?" We then ask two final questions: "What personality skills or characteristics will you most enjoy, and as a result, look for in a potential marriage partner?" "What skills—if missing—would create a problem if not present in a potential partner? Are there skills or traits in a potential partner that, if not present, would make it difficult to live the way you want to?"

Summarize on paper what your teen views as the most important points discussed in your conversation. Encourage your teen to add to the list if there are other skills or traits he considers important—for example, if there are certain sports or activities he would like to share with his lifetime partner/friend. Upon closer examination, these additional traits or skills usually fit one or more of the twelve personality skills. After completing this written overview, sign and date the document—and have your teen do the same. As part of the process, agree with your teen to reevaluate the document and the issues discussed each year through the twelfth grade.

Note: For more adventuresome parents, have a discussion with your teen about how your personality skills match up with his.

Helping Teens Choose Friends and Free-Time Activities

In working through the previous exercise with your teen, you now can see the possibilities when it comes to helping him make better friendship choices. The process of choosing a suitable marriage partner—who will be a lifetime friend—matches the selection process for all friends. If a friend is fun to be with, and if he has similar skills and enjoys the same kind of activities as you do, it generally means that you are compatible with that person. As the selection process for marriage partners and friends is similar, we use steps similar to those in the previous exercise when helping our teen choose enjoyable friends:

Help your teen identify her strongest skills—especially considering the twelve discussed earlier.

Ask your teen to think about the people she knows—in school, in the neighborhood, and among relatives—who might possess similar skills. Identifying even one or two similar skills or traits in another person is a great start.

Guide your teen in discerning which of the potential friends might not be emotionally mature, honest, caring, or responsible. Help her identify the people who do not have desired characteristics as a friend.

Help your teen establish and support a potential friendship. Let her choose someone identified in the first three steps of this exercise. Invite the new friend over, and encourage your teen and the new friend to do things together. In other words, offer practical and emotional support to help cultivate your teen's friendship(s).

As a parent, you also can help your teen evaluate her skills and the activities she enjoys to help identify good choices for free-time activities. Providing your own input—particularly your observations about your teen's talents and the activities she seems to enjoy—is helpful. This is all connected with your teen's God-given skills. By providing concrete help in supporting your teen's free-time choices, you are God's loving instrument in helping meet her needs. In providing this help, you also are practicing the spiritual behavior of servanthood—and modeling for your teen how God-in-Jesus taught us to live as full, vital, loving human beings.

Helping Teens Reach a Career Choice Decision

By now, you possess all the skills you need to help your teen make a wise career choice. The same skills that you and your teen have assessed in the previous exercises to identify friends, desired traits and skills in a future marriage partner, and choices for free-time activities also can be used to point the way toward possible careers. The criteria used to assess a possible career selection will be how well it matches your teen's unique skills, and whether it also would provide job satisfaction, maximum productivity, and career stability.

A helpful tool for the career selection process is the *Occupational Outlook Handbook*, which is published by the U.S. Department of Labor (DOL) and is available at most libraries and major bookstores. The DOL publishes a new issue of the handbook every two years. It provides useful information about the current work environment, necessary education or training, and salaries for all major jobs in the United States.

The Strong Interest Inventory (for ages fourteen and up) is one of the most widely used and accurate tests for making a career choice. It matches your teen's interests with people in more than one hundred twenty work careers. Most psychologists and career centers in junior colleges and universities can provide this test. The results are computer-generated and self-explanatory. Some counselors provide further explanation.

Your Teen's Spirituality

Among all the important parenting skills we have covered so far, helping your teen cultivate his spirituality takes priority. By helping your teen discover who he is, you are helping him fulfill God's plan for life. Recognizing our special gifts and using them in loving service to help others and ourselves allows us to fulfill God's will for our unique contribution to society. From a spiritual standpoint, your teen especially needs help in establishing a personal relationship with God, and in learning to love his neighbor as himself. A parent described to me how his thirteen-year-old son was fidgety in Mass a few years earlier, and how he did not want to be there. Later that summer, the son attended a youth group camp that centered on experiencing a personal relationship with Jesus. Over the next few years, the son became a member of the youth ministry, and eventually, a paid leader of the group. In his adult years, the son eventually owned a retail store. But as owner of the store, the son, his wife, and children developed a loving ministry to serve their urban marginalized customers, while demonstrating a practical way of living and loving their neighbor at the same time. The dad was proud of this son and his family, and said that he wished all teens could have the same opportunity his son did—that is, to be exposed to a personal relationship with Jesus during their early religious training.

Excellent elementary and teen religious education programs in the parish work to help youth develop a personal relationship with Jesus. For example, they emphasize Jesus' presence in all of us, as well as in the Gospels and sacraments. At home, parents also can support the development of a personal connection with Jesus—especially by experiencing the Eucharist together.

One parent mentioned how the entire family would shop for groceries, and then head to the Indian reservation to bring bags of food to the convent so it could be distributed to families in need. In this family, the teens were in charge of organizing this "love your neighbor" event, with the mom providing support in the form of transportation.

Teens also need parental help in learning how to love themselves as instruments of God's love—not only in service to others, but also to self. The earlier exercises, designed to help teens make the correct choices in friends, marriage partners, and careers, also can help them learn how to love themselves as God intends. Teens who learn to identify their skills and know who they are experience strong enjoyment, peace, and powerful motivation in their daily lives. When using one's unique skills, individuals live a fruitful life and generally understand God's will for their lives.

Emotional Illness in Teens

The teen years often involve strong emotions as young people struggle with the two major developmental tasks of discovering their identity and gaining acceptance from peers. During these years, many teens experience problems due to personality differences with parents. Some parents believe their own approach to living is the only way. Because of the parent-child turmoil that often arises, there is the potential for development of emotional illness in teens during this time.

Conflict tends to arise when personality differences are present, but emotional illness also can create conflict. More than personality differences, emotional illness can cause a great deal of harm for the individuals involved, as well as for those around them. Emotional illness usually is observed or experienced in three ways from a behavioral standpoint—through irrationality, anxiety, and depression. You may find yourself saying, "Her behavior does not make sense!" If the irrational behavior continues, or even if it occurs just once in a serious situation, the person may need further observation and professional help. Anxiety, excessive worrying, or overconcern are easy to spot. If you ask, "Do you know why you are so anxious?" and the person responds, "No, I don't," you may have a serious situation that requires professional evaluation.

Depression, excessive sadness, or emotional withdrawal at home or elsewhere also is cause for concern. Addiction to alcohol, drugs, gambling, and/or the Internet are serious symptoms of deeper issues that will require professional evaluation.

How do irrationality, anxiety, and depression create conflict in relationships? Usually, these conditions create conflict due to decisions or behaviors they tend to produce. Irrational anger, for example, can lead to physical abuse of a sibling or parent. Anxiety can lead to poor decision-making. Depression can trigger emotional withdrawal from loved ones, who in turn, become depressed or angry.

Knowing the symptoms associated with emotional illness can relieve the stress of getting caught up in another person's irrationality, anxiety, depression, and other related behaviors. Trust your God-given intelligence to spot these potential symptoms. One has the right—and even the obligation—to seek counseling as a way to relieve these symptoms if you observe them—either in yourself or in your teen.

An Exercise in Forgiveness

Parents face many potential sources of conflict with their teens. Aside from possible personality differences, emotional illness, and the presence of sin, sources of conflict also can develop as a result of your teen's search for identity and the need for peer acceptance. For both parents and teens, the need for forgiveness is a given. Sometimes we hurt one another, and reconciliation is needed. The following exercise is the result of my search through the Old and New Testaments for the most effective forgiveness behavior. As a result of this search, I came to believe that reaching out to celebrate the relationship—as demonstrated in the parable of the Prodigal Son—made the most sense. An individual still has the right to prevent harm to oneself in a relationship. But immediately *reaching out* in love when harmed is fundamental and an effective approach. To experience the power of this behavior, do the following exercise with your family:

Gather your family and sit in a circle. Group everyone so that younger children are paired with an older sibling who is at least seven or eight.

The first person in each pair then states a negative description of the other person. The statement must be negative about the other person, but *not true*. "Your hair is all messed up; it looks crazy." "Your nose is bright red today; it looks awful." "I heard you were bad yesterday." "Your teeth are an ugly blue."

The second person in each pair then responds to the negative statement with a positive, relationship-building response. The response does not have to fit the negative statement. Here are some possibilities: "Your hair looks gorgeous today!" "Your nose so fits your lovely face!" "You have such lovely teeth!"

After saying something positive, the second person then hugs the first person.

The second person restarts the process by making a negative statement to the first person. The first individual then responds with a positive statement, and hugs the second person.

One of the parents or an older child then reminds everyone that the act of reaching out in a positive way after we are harmed is how we can practice forgiveness. When harmed by another person, we simply love her back. We find a creative, special way to build up our relationship with the person who has harmed us.

Chapter Five

Grandparenting

Our morning schedule began with story hour at the library, followed by selecting a few books to fill our red canvas bag. Then my five-year-old granddaughter and I headed to the park to climb the huge wood and plastic jungle gym, with all its slides and tunnels. Lunch at McDonald's came next in her plan, which included still more tunnel time there at the restaurant. My granddaughter loved to organize other children for the next adventure. We then continued on to the Target store so she could pick out one small toy to take home, along with the two McDonald's toys that came with our Happy Meals.

These weekly adventures provided this Grandpa with untold delight. The difficulty came when my granddaughter entered all-day kindergarten. Such a loss! The end of our Wednesdays together triggered some depression in me. We settled for dinner with the family as often as possible. The following summer, we were back to our regular Wednesdays with a new schedule she planned for us. God is so good to me!

Unconditional Love

The thrill of grandparenting is a theological mystery. In older age do we suddenly discover the adult childhood Jesus is calling us to? In rediscovering our youth with help from our grandchildren, do we feel called to practice unconditional love and experience its value? Unconditional love may explain why we become so ready to meet every pressing need of our grandchildren, while passing along some of our own wise values and love for certain activities like books and reading at the same time. Servanthood—described by Jesus as becoming like a little child—requires constant attention so that we can meet our grandchildren's needs. Unconditional love also describes servanthood.

If I approach time with my grandchild with the attitude of servanthood, I am able to listen to her needs and respond to them. This again is unconditional love—total responsiveness with little questioning of motives or values. The love returned from the grandchild also provides additional motivation. The grandparent models the primary behavior God wants all of us to practice, and the grandchild demonstrates that "love for one another" behavior by returning it to us.

Struggles for Control and Who Is Loved Most

Sometimes—despite the unconditional love and servanthood that grandparents demonstrate—they can experience struggles for control with the child's parents. This type of conflict is the most common example of the negative side of grandparenting—not only for the grandparents themselves, but also for the parents and the child. Where does this struggle for control come from? Most often, it originates with the natural personality skill of decision-making. Grandparents with leadership skills often want to impose their judgment. Leadership-oriented parents want their way to prevail in the situation. The struggle for control comes into play when both parents and grandparents try to have their way. Should the grandparents regularly give gifts to their grandchild? Should the child have a later bedtime than the parents are allowing? Why can't the child be better behaved? Why won't the grandparents stop rewarding good behavior with M&M's?

Examples of grandparents contradicting parents on matters like discipline and other child-rearing issues are too numerous to detail here. This struggle for control in the presence of the children is harmful—it can create confusion, make them feel responsible for the conflict, and even have a negative impact on their self-esteem. What does a struggle for control accomplish where grandparents are concerned? Some may find relief from the guilt they feel from raising their own children poorly. In other instances, the struggle for control may provide the grandparent with a sense of power, which from a psychological standpoint may help offset their lack of self-esteem. Nevertheless, parenting remains the primary responsibility of the mother and father. However, parenting issues that involve serious child endangerment are another matter entirely.

The exercise at the end of this chapter can provide an antidote for these struggles for control between parents and grandparents.

Grandparents also may find themselves embroiled in another kind of conflict. Sometimes struggles revolve around the question of who is most loved by a grandchild. Sometimes, grandparents may struggle to prove that their grandchild loves them more than their parents. Why such a contest? Insecurities related to self-worth often are at the root of such a conflict. An emotionally healthy grandparent can kid around about it: "Of course I'm more special!" Healthy grandparents work hard to make sure their grandchildren know the many ways their parents love them, and why the parents should be the primary focus of their grandchildren's love.

Balancing Solutions Against Causes of Conflict

Sources of conflict, including natural personality differences, emotional illness, and sin, exist in grandparent relationships as everywhere else. The grandparent-parent control issue represents the most common source of conflict, but many others also can arise. A grandparent may simply enjoy one grandchild's personality more than another's—perhaps due to a closer match of personality skills and traits. A parent may enjoy one grandparent more than another for the same reason. As in marriage, servanthood can provide a solution and help ease a considerable amount of stress. When relating to a grandparent with fewer personality skills in common, for example, the parent can acknowledge those personality differences and honor that grandparent's stronger need to be in charge. This can mean listening to contrary opinions out of love for a grandparent who has a need to be in charge, while consciously withholding judgments or opinions on unimportant issues. Individuals can find a wide variety of creative ways to practice loving servanthood in these relationships.

Emotional illness, which can exist in grandparents, grandchildren, or parents, also can be a source of conflict. Servanthood, however, can help alleviate causes of low self-esteem, as well as irrationality, anxiety, depression, and other symptoms and behaviors that can accompany emotional illness. As discussed in Chapter Three, forgiveness also can prove helpful in positive, loving outreach behavior. When dealing with symptoms associated with emotional illness, you can find peace of mind by using your intellect to ask questions about the other person's behavior. The most basic question is, "Does this behavior make sense?" Along with trusting your own judgment, answering this question can help you achieve some peace of mind. When dealing with illnesses like Alzheimer's disease and dementia, this kind of questioning can help keep you more at peace.

In other instances, sin can create serious conflict. Out of extreme self-interest, grandparents, parents, or others sometimes do grave harm to a child or to each other. Lying, theft, endangering a grand-child, physical violence, use of drugs, and many other behaviors need to be stopped or kept at a distance from children. Use of the intellect to identify sin and how to deal with it also can provide a major help. At times, speaking out about the sinful behavior may be part of the solution.

Finding Talents in Grandchildren

Once children reach the age of reason, grandparents can confidently guide children in thinking about their unique talents. The following is an effective two-question scenario:

"Rachel, what did you most enjoy this past year in first grade?"

"Arts and crafts, Grandma."

"And what do you want to be when you grow up?"

"A mother and a ballerina teacher, Grandma," says Rachel, who does a pirouette.

From this brief exchange, we have learned that Rachel may well have artistic talent based on her mention of ballet and arts and crafts. Rachel's desire to be a mother and teacher may originate from her talent for nurturing, decision-making, and leadership. Grandma can help Rachel by sharing these observations with her.

For example, Grandma might say, "Rachel, you are really good at arts and crafts, and I think you would make a great mom and ballerina teacher."

Questions like, "What do you enjoy?" and "What do you want to be when you grow up?" help identify an individual's talents. At the homeless shelter where I do volunteer career counseling, I regularly ask people who are fifty and older what they wanted to be when they were six or seven years old. Their answers often are in line with results from the extensive career testing I do to help them identify their unique talents.

Modeling Growing Old

On the positive side of grandparenting, there is the opportunity to model how to grow old gracefully. Building family culture in one's remaining years is one way to do that. Other possibilities may present themselves in answer to this question: What are the values you would like to leave behind for the family? Service to those in need? Education? Enjoyment of the outdoors? Solid financial stability? Enjoyment of the arts? Family get-togethers? Church volunteerism? You can leave this kind of legacy behind by building these values in your own life, modeling the behavior you want to see continue in your family, and by involving your grandchildren as much as possible. One wonderful, wealthy man I know created a trust fund to help the needy all over the world. As part of his gift, he had his children and grandchildren take management responsibility for each charity associated with that fund, including oversight of the people impacted by the fund.

Grandparents also can model some of the previously discussed behavior solutions to help manage conflict and stress. By example, grandparents can teach others in the family how to respond in a loving way toward others who have unique personalities and needs. Grandparents also can model how to respond in a positive way and with an attitude of forgiveness to the harmful words and actions of other family members. Offering useful insights when family members are confronted with problems, and speaking out on behalf of others in the family who are mistreated also are ways that grandparents can have a positive influence on grandchildren and other family members.

By example, grandparents also can model how to deal with advancing age and the loss of physical health. Do they complain? Do they spend too much time describing their ills? Do they act irritated and depressed? Do they let others do what they could do for themselves? Or do they joke around about how long it takes them to walk around or about their need for a cane? Do they always seem upbeat and concentrate on what others are doing and saying? And as their illness progresses, do they demonstrate their trust in God's love and peaceful care?

Early Retirement Can Bury One's Talents

Grandparents need to beware of burying their talents with the inertia and inactivity that sometimes accompany early retirement. As we draw closer to the ultimate encounter with our Maker, the parable about talents should give us pause. Our later years are as important as our middle years in the way we serve others with the unique talents our Master has given us. Even in retirement, those talents must continue to earn interest. Jesus told the story about the master specifically condemning the person who buried his one and only talent. "You wicked, lazy servant!…Should you not then have put my money in the bank…" (Matthew 25:26–27). We live in a time when many grandparents are still able to be productive well into their mid-eighties, and even into their mid-nineties. Regardless of our age, our talents still need to be drawing interest through continuous use.

Early retirement that is marked by inactivity in serving others, and by only playing golf and watching television, does not fit into the Christian ethic. In fact, with today's economic pressures, many choose to remain in the workforce. Volunteerism also provides many productive outlets with opportunities to draw on one's unique talents. Grandchildren also need all the great memories their grandparents can creatively provide them. Through grandparents' love, children experience God's love and learn to appreciate how special they are.

Old Age and Use of the Intellect

Research shows that cognitive abilities tend to remain intact the longest. Physical, social, and behavioral abilities often degenerate more rapidly—much like what Pope John Paul II experienced. Despite dealing with the debilitating effects of Parkinson's disease, he remained an extraordinary model for all of us as he continued to intelligently run the universal Church. Most are aware that staying active intellectually through reading and various forms of problem-solving helps ward off Alzheimer's disease and the buildup of plaque in the brain.

From a theological perspective, it comes as no surprise that the intellect—the primary power of our soul along with our will—would continue to function the longest. Staying active intellectually by remaining curious, asking questions, and looking for solutions makes life more interesting and also can be used in loving service to others.

Being Cared For and Final Preparations

My grandmother, the matriarch of our family, lived to be 105 years old. Despite her age, she actively belonged to bridge clubs until the very end. Whenever we gathered together as an extended family, I remember the way she helped me with some of my own life situations through her strength and humorous wisdom. She peacefully accepted having to be cared for. After she broke her hip several months before passing away, my grandmother gave the visiting pastor a hard time for not bringing her a cold beer. I still treasure the ancient leather-bound Bible she passed on to me a few years before her death. Most of all, she was a positive example to us. As part of her legacy, she left us with her dedication to Church, her humorous wisdom, and the peaceful way she dealt with old age.

What are some questions we can ask ourselves when we are being cared for and when it is clear that we must confront our own passing? Here are a few possibilities:

"What are the needs of my caregivers, and is there a way I can help them?"

"How can I be of service to other members of my extended family, friends, and others?" "What talents must I be careful not to bury?"

"Am I ready to meet my Maker?"

"Who still needs my forgiveness for hurts, or recompense for harm I have caused?"

"What do I still need to speak up about regarding my own needs and the needs of others?"

"How can I grow in my personal love relationship with God?"

Summary of Practical Applications

* When spending time with your grandchildren, pay attention to the experience of having a second childhood and the process of becoming more childlike in the way that Jesus called us to do.

* Practice unconditional love and experience its value.

* Be attentive to your grandchildren's needs at the same time that you are passing along some of your wisdom and values in life.

* Model attention to your grandchildren's needs, but also state your own so that they learn from your example how to respond with loving attention to others' needs.

* Help maintain your grandchildren's understanding that their parents are the ones who love them most.

* Recognize that it is natural for a grandparent to enjoy one grand-child more than another as a result of having more skills and traits in common.

* Attend to the needs of the grandchildren who may not have as much in common with you—it provides an opportunity for servanthood.

✳ Practice servanthood to help lessen the anxiety and low self-esteem that can accompany emotional illness.

✳ Use your intellect by asking questions in identifying sin in others and how to deal with it.

✳ Speaking out against sinful behavior sometimes is needed in family and other situations.

✳ Help your grandchildren identify their talents by asking them what they enjoy doing most and what they want to be when they grow up.

✳ Model the values you would like to leave behind as part of your family's culture.

✳ Teach your grandchildren and adult children how to resolve conflict and stress by example. Model how to respond with love to the needs of family members and others, as well as how to practice forgiveness. Useful problem-solving and speaking out when others are mistreated also are behaviors to teach by example.

✳ Be upbeat and concentrate on the needs of others even as you experience illness and declining health.

✳ Express your trust in God's love and peaceful care if your illness becomes more serious.

✳ Do volunteer work at church that is a good match with your talents.

✳ Demonstrate that one's later years are just as important as the middle years when it comes to using one's unique talent in the service of others.

✳ Ask yourself how you can set aside time daily to grow in attention to God by reflecting on Scripture and talking to God.

Exercise on Struggles for Control

The two primary tools for resolving conflict between two decision-makers also can help resolve conflict between parents and grandparents:

Listen to the other person's reasoning to better understand her point of view, and to shed light on contrary judgments you are making in the situation. In doing this, both parties can exercise their talents and abilities as leaders and decision-makers.

Allow the parents to make the final decision on issues since they have primary responsibility for their child. The grandparent can have his or her say, but in every instance, it is helpful to remember that the primary and final responsibility remains with the parents. Taking this approach also leaves the door open for parents to decide that the grandparent's rationale makes more sense after all. Otherwise, the parent may respond by heading in an irrational direction—just to prove that his approach is the better one.

Chapter Six

Problems and Solutions Regarding Sexuality

Counseling seven hundred engaged couples at the Franciscan Retreat Center left me with a clear awareness of the many problems related to sexuality. First was the statistic that at least half of these Catholic couples were already living together. Another was my discovery from the testing process that at least half of the couples had personality differences that could result in divorce, regardless of what they viewed as a satisfying sexual relationship. Most disturbing was discovering that couples who had even just one similar personality skill or trait in common, such as being highly sociable, could trigger the emotion of falling in love. Based on those in-love feelings and the sense that they had found the right person, many couples already were involved in a sexual relationship, with all the bonding power of that kind of relationship. At the same time, many couples ignored serious negative personality traits and differences that were strong indicators of trouble and possible divorce down the road. The solutions to these and other problems related to sexuality include the four solution behaviors discussed in previous chapters.

The Power and Value of Sexuality

The power of sexuality remains a constant in human history, and in each of our personal lives. The authors of Genesis rightly dealt with that power in the opening stories of our religious history. "The LORD God said: "It is not good for the man to be alone. I will make a suitable partner for him" (Genesis 2:18). "That is why a man leaves his father and mother and clings to his wife, and the two of them become one body" (Genesis 2:24). "…male and female he created them…'Be fertile and multiply…'" (Genesis 1:27–28). One of the most fascinating descriptions of the human race is this: "God created man in his image; in the divine image he created him; male and female he created them" (Genesis 1:27). Somehow our sexuality reflects God's own most powerful, productive, and bonding love.

Understanding and accepting the power of human sexuality provides foundational wisdom that facilitates how to rationally deal with that power. This power is derived from the attraction and enjoyment that naturally is built into our sexuality. God's plan to provide ways of bonding and multiplying into our sexuality was successful. Our acceptance of this reality, along with making rational decisions to control that power, ensures that it will work properly for us. God gives us tools—like our intellect and will—that by their very nature are more powerful than the physical drive of human sexuality. We will discuss how to use these tools to address problems related to sexuality.

Knowing the value of sexuality helps to control it. The peace and bonding derived from its initiation and completion meet deep human needs. However, logic suggests that there are additional ways to meet those same needs. For example, any compatible friendship without sexuality also can provide peace and human bonding. The majority of married people who responded to the U.S. bishops' 2007–2008 National Pastoral Institute Survey on marriage answered "soulmate" as a major factor in human sexuality. That same kind of sharing and bonding also is possible in a non-sexual relationship between good friends.

Procreation requires sexuality. But there are other ways to enjoy children—through adoption, grandparenting, and getting involved with relatives and friends who have children.

As for the spiritual values of sexuality, the intensity of human affection and physical enjoyment is a model for our love union with God—much as Solomon expresses in his "Canticle of Canticles." The total surrender of self in giving and receiving love is a natural part of sexuality. Enjoying God's best physical creation in the midst of the bonding of two human spirits can bring thanksgiving and appreciation of God's power and beauty. At the heart of this is the experience of a loving relationship, which God calls us to in many ways through spirituality, and as witnessed by the lives of so many priests, religious, and single lay people.

Personality Attraction Problems and Solutions

As noted earlier, engaged couples often experience problems related to sexuality. For many couples, relationship problems stem from the natural attraction that often accompanies compatible talents or skills. For example, Jill enjoys the attention she receives from John when he asks for her help in making a workplace decision. This interaction eventually leads to dating, and to other explorations related to their growing love. But as they begin to experience sexual desires, Jill and John decide to wait until they are able to determine the relationship will work as a marriage.

The following questions can help determine whether a couple's initial personality attraction and in-love feelings are enduring enough to consider marriage. As part of this exercise, each person should ask:

* "Am I strongly attracted to or in love with this person?"
* "What do I most enjoy about the other person?" (See Chapter Two on talents.)
* "What do I *not* enjoy about the other person and her behaviors?"
* "Can I live with the person's positive and negative behaviors and traits for a lifetime?"

Pay attention to your instinctive answer to the fourth question. Whether it's a "no" or a "yes," you are probably getting the answer from your intellect, which God uses to lead you to the truth. The accuracy of your answer hinges on how thorough you are in assessing the other person and her behaviors. More time may be needed to get to know one another. There always is the possibility that one or both people may be hiding their true nature to please and conform to the other person.

You can experience what it's like to receive an answer from your intellect by following these steps:

✳ Develop a list of names of people you have been attracted to in the past, and in considering each one, ask yourself: "Would I have enjoyed living with that person's personality behaviors for a lifetime?"

✳ Consider the answers you have received by asking this question. Hopefully they will demonstrate that your judgment can be accurate—especially when you ask yourself "Why?" for each of your "no" answers.

The above process can generate uncertainty and errors in judgment. But by asking these questions, the intellect is forced to work with the facts it gathers in the process. God judges us according to our effort, not on the accuracy of the answers. Regular prayer and asking God to strengthen your will and bring clarity to your intellect throughout the process all are important. After taking these steps, trust in God's love for you and your partner as you separately make a decision about whether to continue your relationship in marriage.

Parenting and Commitment

After receiving the marriage sacrament, free-flowing sexuality provides beauty, enjoyment, excitement, bonding, and peace, as designed by God. While sexuality has its own simple pattern of stimulation and completion, the advice of a family physician or counselor can provide helpful sexual variety through books and other resources.

Child-rearing absorbs a lot of energy and attentiveness over a span of years. But smart parents learn to make time for each other in a number of ways, including through the beauty and peace of their sexual experiences. Lock the bedroom door. Create opportunities to spend time together—even for a day—with help from grandparents, other relatives, or friends who are willing to watch your children. Even after setting time aside for each other, there may be the temptation to say, "I'm too tired." While this may be true, following through on plans to spend time together may provide an opportunity for one or both parents to practice servanthood or to have a discussion about better distribution of childcare tasks.

The demands of child-rearing, job-related pressures, and growing dissatisfaction due to personality differences can create a situation where other relationships may hold some attraction. But that attraction is no different than what one probably experienced while falling in love with one's spouse. The experience of falling in love often is triggered by just one natural personality similarity. The rush of feelings and thoughts like "This person is the only one for me" or "This relationship will last forever" can challenge a person's commitment to their current marriage.

The following can be danger signals to a spouse and indicators that your marital commitment is being challenged:

You may:

* Give gifts to a new interest of yours.
* Want to spend an unnecessary amount of time with that person.
* Spend a lot of time praising this other person.
* Experience strong feelings of attraction that do not go away.
* Some possible remedies for this situation include:
* Understanding that these feelings come from natural personality compatibilities, and that only one area of compatibility is needed to trigger them.

✻ Asking the obvious question: "Is pursuing this attraction a challenge to my commitment to my spouse?" Ask yourself any other questions that will force your intellect to discover truth about the situation.

✻ Praying for strength to follow through on what you know to be the right course of action—especially when answers to your questions are telling you not to pursue the attraction.

✻ Separating emotionally and physically from the other person until the feelings of attraction feelings are gone. Hopefully, you have not shared your feelings with that other person.

✻ Recommitting yourself to enjoying all the things you have enjoyed in your spouse from the beginning, including your sexual relationship.

Adultery committed simply for the sake of variety in sexual experience is a less common temptation, and could signal a much deeper personality disorder. Such behavior breaks the marriage bond, as does any natural personality attraction that ends in sexual union. An emotionally stable and moral person can make a sound moral decision to resist these temptations. Even so, it's always necessary to pray and trust in God for the grace needed to strengthen your intellect and will.

Adolescents and Sex

After counseling teens for twenty-five years, I still find adolescent sexuality to be one of the most challenging issues to deal with. As mentioned earlier, the primary developmental tasks during the teen years are to discover one's identity and to find social acceptance among one's peers. A parent's best hope of keeping teens on the right path sexually lies in getting involved in these developmental tasks.

A helpful start can begin with parents acknowledging their own sexual behavior during their teen years. They can then ask themselves, "What would be the best behavior—and make the most sense—in dealing with sexuality as a teenager? Why is this the best behavior?" From this exploration, parents can create a positive, intelligent approach to present to their teens. And they can challenge their teens to develop their own best image of who they want to be in life, including who they want to be as a sexual human being.

Secondly, parents do have the power to influence their teen's choice of friends. They can exercise this power by actively supporting friendships that appear to be emotionally and morally healthy for their teen. Offering your teen input regarding natural personality compatibilities as discussed in Chapter Four on parenting teens also can be helpful. By providing this input, you increase the likelihood of success in your efforts to promote the right friends for your teen. The advice offered earlier in this chapter on how to manage natural personality attractions and handle the experience of falling in love also can be beneficial. This advice also can be used when dealing with attraction toward young and older adults.

Teaching teens to use their intellect by asking questions is a powerful tool that can be used to help manage sexual behavior—even when strong emotions and urges surface, as they tend to do at this age. Teens need to ask common-sense questions like, "What impact will this behavior have on my self-image in the future?" and, "What would this behavior cost me and others now and in the future?"

Encourage your teen to share feelings and problems with you. Foster frank discussions about their values, emotions, and any problems they are experiencing related to sexuality. As a parent, having these discussions early is important. In fact, today's statistics show that sexual involvement often begins as early as middle school. While not desirable, ignorance may protect some teens for a time. But given the fact that half of today's high school students are sexually active, the odds are slim that ignorance will protect them for very long.

Children who grow up in a family-based culture of service to others have an added advantage as they enter their teenage years. Teens who have had the opportunity to practice being an instrument of God's love to themselves and others are more inclined to seek only legitimate good in their relationships and other situations. Those who learn how to practice forgiveness also have an advantage when they enter their teen years. For example, teens who harbor unforgiving anger toward their parents may be tempted to do the opposite of what their parents want them to do—including making poor decisions related to sexual involvement.

As I mentioned earlier, adolescent sexuality is one of the most challenging areas to deal with as a counselor. But there are tools that parents and teens can use to effectively deal with challenges that surface during the teen years. The greatest source of strength and light for parents and teens can be found by regularly attending Mass.

Value of Friendships

Married couples who focus on developing their friendships are better able to control their sexuality and remain faithful in their marriages. True friendship—which seeks only good for the other person—precludes violence, infidelity, and withholding of sexual relations in a marriage.

Bonding, understanding, enjoyment, and peace often are found at the heart of the sexual experience. In a similar but much different way, the bonds of friendship can foster mutual understanding, enjoyment, and peace. Living as a Marianist Brother for ten years, I can attest to the fact that friendships within my community of fellow religious made it possible to live out the vow of celibacy. This truth became clear to me when I learned that the vow of celibacy does not result in an increase in special graces compared to those who choose to live chaste lives as single or married individuals. Though the Benedictine rule of silence was our way of life as Marianists, the hour of "free recreation" time following dinner, the communal prayer life of Mass, and other occasions made bonding in friendship possible. Healthy, natural friendships can aid chastity in any walk of life—whether living as a religious or as a lay person.

One of the most noteworthy conversations in Jesus' ministry took place at Jacob's well when he asked the Samaritan woman for a drink of water. Jesus asked her to bring her husband to the well, and come back for further conversation. When the Samaritan woman told Jesus she had no husband, Jesus said: "…you have had five husbands, and the one you have now is not your husband" (John 4:18). In responding to her apparent search for a better relationship in life, Jesus reveals to the Samaritan woman what the human spirit ultimately seeks in human love relationships. "True worshipers will worship the Father in Spirit and truth; and indeed the Father seeks such people to worship him. God is Spirit, and those who worship him must worship in Spirit and truth" (John 4:23–24). All of us need to stay attuned to this call—the invitation to participate in the ultimate love relationship throughout our daily lives.

Exercise: An Examination of One's Own Sexuality

The power of sexuality in the human makeup, and how we feel about that reality in our own lives, can provide helpful information. Asking ourselves a few questions about our own sexuality is the best way to access that information about ourselves. While this exercise is written for individuals, it also can be helpful information to share with your spouse.

* As I experience it, how would I define sexuality?
* Based on my experience, what are some spiritual components or aspects of sexuality?
* What are the positive values I associate with sexuality?
* What are the negative values I associate with sexuality, and is there a solution for those?
* Are there positive decisions that I need to make about my sexuality?

Chapter Seven

Christian Living and Evangelization in the Workplace

Welcome to Ken's Hardware! My name is Ken. What can I help you with this morning?" As Ken extends his hand in friendship, the glaring customer barely glances up as he strides toward a gardening tool display in the main aisle. Trusting that he still might be of help, Ken positions himself near the display, ready to point out where the other gardening tools are located. When the customer appears frustrated after not finding what he's looking for, Ken says: "Let me show you where the rest of our gardening tools are located."

In the above example, Ken bravely tried all four Scripture behaviors in an effort to alleviate potential conflict. Servanthood, forgiveness, use of the intellect, and speaking out provide a grace-filled system of Christian spirituality. They also make for excellent relationship and workplace behaviors. In practicing them, we have the opportunity to do some quiet evangelization by modeling how a Christian is to behave in all relationships—whether at work or home.

Marketing strategists know that responding to customer needs is the most successful approach to marketing. Tuning in to the needs of someone else is key to practicing good servanthood behavior. Forgiving put-downs from immature customers or jealous coworkers gives us the opportunity to overcome the negative realities of most workplace environments. Identifying and meeting customer needs, and responding in a positive way to a negative customer, require intelligent problem-solving. Finally, speaking out assertively to defend a customer, coworker, or yourself also is a workplace behavior that aligns with Christian spirituality.

The Challenge of Personality Differences

Control issues account for most conflicts in the workplace, as well as in other areas of our lives. Since the majority of U.S. businesses are small in size, major decisions often involve a husband and wife, or other business partners. In many cases, business decisions involve two or more natural leaders who are equally gifted in sound judgment, and who want their approach to prevail. As a result, it is not uncommon for one of the people involved to take an irrational stance—just so he or she can be right. In other situations, decision-makers sometimes realize that there are two workable approaches, but continue to debate the merits of each approach *ad infinitum* to prevail in the situation. For more than twenty-five years, I have observed that the God-given skill of decision-making rests in trusting one's own judgment. And while this is necessary for good leadership, it also can carry the risk of regular conflict.

Other personality differences may cause less irritation, anger, and other negative feelings. But as the following examples illustrate, they still can create an unpleasant environment at work. John, who is independent, does not like having a structured schedule. He irritates coworkers who often have to wait for him to show up for his shift. Helen, who is sociable and outgoing, continues to talk to a coworker about her difficult family situation while a customer waits for service. Encountering workplace challenges due to unregulated personality differences is a common problem.

The Challenges of Emotional Illness and Sin

Emotional illness can be difficult to deal with in the workplace—even if an employee has the skills, talent, and know-how to do a job well. However, sometimes behaviors associated with an unregulated emotional illness can interfere with an employee's ability to get the job done. For example, a heavy-drinking cousin who finds himself without a job as the result of another weekend binge may be hired at the family business. Or an uncle—known for his irrational, angry outbursts at his wife and children—is hired at his brother's store.

Job interviewers have to determine whether a candidate has the ability to do the job, work in a responsible way, and work well with others in the company's workplace environment. However, despite a job interviewer's best efforts, employees who engage in damaging behavior sometimes are hired anyway. The employee may perform well for the first few weeks or months, but after a certain amount of time on the job, negative behaviors may begin to surface in the workplace. Some of these troubling behaviors can include stealing, lying, racial slurs, sexual harassment, negative behaviors associated with addiction, slander, and acting out on workplace jealousies. An employee's tendency toward procrastination, laziness, self-indulgence at the expense of others, and lack of financial or other work-related competencies also can have a negative impact on the workplace environment.

Workplace issues also can result from immoral management decisions, including paying unfair wages, sexism, unfair or unhealthy work schedules and demands, false advertising, and unjust profits. Evangelizing the workplace includes playing a role in helping to resolve immoral or troublesome behaviors in the work environment.

Living as a Christian in the Workplace

In looking back over my varied work experiences, the challenges and opportunities for living the Christian life have been endless. These experiences have included working in parish, religious order, and retreat center ministries; participating in national and diocesan training seminars; being a fireman on the Santa Fe Railroad; repossessing cars; throwing newspapers; working in an Ace Hardware nuts and bolts department; and teaching and counseling in high schools and colleges. The challenges I encountered working in all these environments included dealing with behaviors related to natural personality differences, emotional illness, and sin. The opportunities to learn, practice, and teach Christian behaviors were present in all these environments.

In conclusion, I am grateful for having discovered the simplicity, interactive support, and grace-filled power of the four behaviors Jesus practiced while performing his work. Living a full Christian life in any workplace is abundantly possible when dealing with customers and coworkers.

Practicing the Christian Life with Customers

Working at Ozanam Manor—a Saint Vincent de Paul shelter in Phoenix for more than fifty homeless people—brought me closest to what Christian life is all about. As a volunteer career counselor at the shelter, I had several "customers." Of the people who came to the shelter, my customers were the ones chosen to endure up to three hours of the best available career testing to assess their skills and interests. While following up with the test-takers in individual counseling, I discovered that many already had college and postgraduate degrees. Addictions or emotional illness often contributed to their homeless situation.

As I heard one story after another, my heart went out to these people who were experiencing an extraordinary contrast between their prior work lives and their current condition. Many of them held onto hope by the tiniest of threads. Yet they were God's beloved children, and they were open to receiving any available help to put their lives back in order. With all its professional and volunteer services, Ozanam Manor was there to provide that hope. God—by using others as instruments of his love—was taking care of "the least of our brethren." I was impressed with many of the people who walked through the doors of the shelter. Most were in the middle of a poverty experience, and they were discovering what it was like to have nothing in our culture. Despite their condition, however, many were able to receive the ultimate gift—the grace of understanding that life is all about the relationship we have with God.

More often, however, the customers who came to the shelter were looking to have their basic needs met. They needed food, clothing, housing, medical help, legal assistance, gas, and car repairs. In helping to meet these needs, others had the opportunity to share their talents and provide for their own needs. Many jobs—like those in the sales and service industries—provide opportunities for Christians to practice servanthood by loving and serving others.

Being able to forgive hurts caused by others also is a needed behavior when working in customer service jobs. People who work in service-oriented jobs often are confronted with customers who seem to view and treat them as nothing more than servants. As a result, some customers do not view those who work in service-oriented positions as equals, or as brothers and sisters. So customers sometimes treat workers poorly—as if theirs are the only needs that matter. As a result, people working in jobs that require a lot of customer contact sometimes have to endure customers' irrational, angry outbursts; racist and sexist remarks; and other negative behaviors.

Business owners also must contend with customers' occasional bad behavior. For example, business owners sometimes have to forgive serious infractions, like theft. But the best Christian response to all hurtful behavior that originates with customers resides in the attempt to reach out and build a positive relationship with the offender. Other behaviors—like speaking out to defend oneself or the business—also are legitimate responses when good judgment calls for them.

Though some may challenge the use of intellect as a spiritual behavior in the workplace, both logic and theology affirm the need for its presence and use. In fact, the love relationships we have with God and others are a function of the soul, as well as powers of the intellect and will. By its very nature, the life of grace that God gives us assists our intellect and our will. Proper use of the intellect is a central behavior in spirituality. It provides us with the power to arrive at the truth, solve problems, discern what is good and bad behavior before God, and judge how and when to practice servanthood, forgiveness, and speaking out.

Throughout our daily work life, use of the intellect also keeps us connected with God. We ask for God's help, and we give thanks for that assistance in our search for solutions to deal with customer needs and idiosyncrasies. In addition, we think about how we might be better able to help improve profits and reenvision the services our business provides. The opportunities to improve all aspects of our workplace are endless when we ask ourselves and our customers questions.

Practicing the Christian Life With Coworkers

During the summers of my first college years, I worked as a freight train fireman on the Santa Fe Railroad. My coworkers were the only associations I had during those summer months. We would pull ninety-nine cars full of cantaloupe from Phoenix up to the Northern Arizona mountain's Chicago-to-L.A. mainline. The engineer and I would share the wonders of Arizona mountain scenery together, including the antelopes who would keep pace alongside our lead diesel on flat stretches. During our trek, we often would trade humorous comments like, "Do you think the antelopes know this is a cantaloupe train?" This kind of camaraderie met our socializing needs during the times we worked together on the train.

While working for the railroad, I noticed on one of the runs that everyone was shunning a particular brakeman. I later found out that the man—to protect his wife and children financially—had crossed a union picket line. The engineer I worked with understood the man's rationale for doing what he did, but the engineer still joined his colleagues in their years of silent disapproval of the brakeman. They held onto their silence for the sake of maintaining union solidarity—their only hope of dealing with potentially unjust corporate practices. But in the process, they also turned away from the opportunity to reach out in forgiveness to this man. They traded forgiveness for the larger reality they felt they had to preserve, and they spoke out by giving this coworker the silent treatment.

Daily opportunities for forgiveness, servanthood, use of the intellect, and speaking out are abundant every day in the workplace and in the relationships we have with our coworkers. But even though many opportunities present themselves on a daily basis, we must watch and act on them when they present themselves to us.

Evangelizing Customers and Coworkers

Recently, I asked a salesman in his late twenties: "Would you be offended if I, as a Catholic, worked here at your store and tried to evangelize you to my faith just by modeling Christian behaviors—not by talking about my faith?" This bright, sociable, unchurched, and independent young man responded with a quick "No!" He also said that he would be offended if anyone tried to verbally preach to him: "Who does he think he is, trying to tell me what to believe?" In other words, he considered independence of choice critical to one's rights as a person.

In this chapter, we have discussed the many opportunities to act with Christian behavior toward customers and coworkers. Many issues also call for a Christian approach or solution to resolve problems in the workplace. By practicing the four Christian behaviors of forgiveness, servanthood, use of the intellect, and speaking out in our own lives, we also can evangelize the workplace by modeling those behaviors for others around us. In this way, Christian evangelization can help people know and live out a personal relationship with God. Using Jesus' four behaviors can have a powerful impact on the workplace. These four behaviors:

✳ Can alleviate conflict and stress in the workplace.

✳ Are needed in the workplace to maintain a healthy, functioning environment.

✳ Can help us evangelize if we model them in our interactions with customers and coworkers in the workplace.

Evangelizing can play an integral role in our daily work life. When we focus on listening and responding to the legitimate needs of customers and coworkers, we are evangelizing them. We are letting them experience how God loves them, and also how we as Catholics love them. By modeling these behaviors we also are showing them by example how positive and useful this behavior could be if they chose to practice forgiveness, servanthood, use of the intellect, and speaking out in their own work life.

Matching One's Skills With Workplace Needs

Serving the needs of others is the primary behavior of living as a Christian in the workplace. Serving your own needs happens when you choose a job, a career, and a work environment that are well-matched with who you are, what you like to do, and your skills and talents. If you love to socialize, that need is met when you are able to do that day after day where you work. By choosing work that matches your predominant skills, and that allows you to do what you most enjoy, you are exercising servanthood toward yourself. Jesus called us to love ourselves as we love our neighbor. Matching our talents (covered in Chapter Two) with the needs of the job we are intended to perform is a key step in practicing our Christian faith in the workplace. When we do work we enjoy, the joy and productivity we experience are in alignment with Jesus in Matthew 5:16: "Your light must shine before others, that they may see your good deeds and glorify your heavenly Father."

An Exercise for Measuring One's Growth in the Four Behaviors

We have explored four behaviors that Jesus used when dealing with conflict in his own life. The following exercise will help measure and motivate progress in our Christian way of life and how we evangelize in the workplace.

The following questions can help you evaluate your progress on a weekly basis:

A. Practicing loving servanthood
   1. How has my attitude demonstrated a growing awareness of and attraction to the unique qualities of loving goodness that God has instilled in each person?

   2. In what ways am I improving my attentiveness to the needs of others through observation, listening, and questioning? Where have I found opportunities to humbly respond to the needs of others, including the "least of my brethren"?

B. Practicing forgiveness
   1. In what situations have I maintained a loving attitude despite hurtful or harmful behavior from a customer or coworker? In doing so, have I reminded myself of the inherent goodness that God has granted each individual?

   2. When I have experienced hurtful behavior from someone else, how have I responded? Have I thought of and carried out an action to build up a positive friendship between us?

C. Practicing use of the intellect
   1. Have I recently asked myself questions like, "What good qualities can I find and enjoy in this person?" In asking this and other similar questions, has my loving attitude increased toward others?

   2. When have I used questions to discover and serve my own needs and the needs of others? When have I used questions to find out the "why" in situations as a way to facilitate forgiveness of others? How have I used questions in the process of speaking out?

D. Practicing speaking out:
   1. How am I growing in my ability to speak out in situations without hurting others, and without letting pride get in the way?

   2. When have I effectively spoken out on behalf of my own or others' needs? When have I spoken out to build up friendship during the process of forgiveness?

Chapter Eight

Sickness and Suffering in Family Life

At the age of three, I stood on the far side of my mother's bed and watched her fix her hat in the mirror, getting ready to go somewhere. This memory is the only and last image I have of my mother. She was twenty-four and probably getting ready to go to the hospital, where she soon died from a brain tumor. When I was sixty years old, I had a second close encounter with death—I came within thirty minutes of dying from a burst appendix.

Relatives have told me how traumatized I was by my mother's death. The second incident left me both angry and grateful. I was angry at the difficulty I experienced while getting checked into the emergency room. But I was grateful that I had stopped at the hospital to get a growing stomach pain checked out before leaving for a week-long camping trip in the Sierra Mountains. Where was God in these life-and-death experiences?

Sickness and Suffering from a Loving God?

When faced with sickness, suffering, and death, we sometimes wonder how a loving God can allow these things to happen to us. We do not want our loved ones to suffer, get sick, or die. At times, we may blame ourselves for not taking the right action to avoid our own illnesses. If we spend an hour suffering in a dentist's chair, for example, we may wonder why we ignored self-care by not flossing more regularly. When we face unavoidable sickness, suffering, or death in our lives or in the lives of others, we may instinctively blame God. We may find ourselves asking, "How can God do this to us?" In situations where innocent children face sickness or death, we find ourselves particularly challenged to understand why. We may ask ourselves, "Where is this loving God now?"

The answer to these questions can be found at the foundation of our faith. God's love for us is total and all-encompassing. God does not want sickness, suffering, or death. Even in Scripture, we see Jesus weeping as he witnesses the sisters of Lazarus mourn his death. Jesus then raises Lazarus from the dead, perhaps to demonstrate how God does not want to see death or the suffering it causes for anyone. Throughout Scripture, we witness Jesus performing miracles to help the blind see, the lepers heal, and the crippled walk. Miracles come from God. But sometimes—as in Jesus' case—suffering and death happen anyway. God permitted Jesus to suffer at the hands of evil men instead of performing a miracle to save him. The evil did not come from God—it came from Pharisee leaders, who through their own free will, chose to kill Jesus.

First Cause: The Nature of Material Things

God the Father could have kept sickness, suffering, and death from the human experience. God did this in the Garden of Eden, and God does it for all those in heaven for the rest of eternity. But while we are on earth, God allows the human experience and the rest of physical creation to be what they are in the natural order of things. We see the natural order of things all around us—things in our physical world change and degrade *because* they are physical. The rose on the bush blossoms dies—and in the process, it leaves behind seeds that will grow into new bushes. Trees lose their leaves in the fall, then grow new ones in the spring. Human bodies eventually wear out, or are unable to heal after surviving traumatic injury. The heart and blood vessels sometimes wear out or stop functioning as a result of high cholesterol and other conditions. Examples like this are endless because they are part of the reality of the physical world around us. And God allows this world to function, as it is—a physical world.

During a three-day visit at Lourdes in France, I was reminded that miracles do not happen in the natural order of things. God does not usually bypass the normal and logical functioning of the physical world by performing miracles. Four million people visit the shrine at Lourdes every year, and everyone who goes there experiences God's presence in some way. Many people who are seriously ill choose to undergo an evaluation at the hospital before and after experiencing the baths, Mass, or the blessings of Benediction at Lourdes. In these evaluations, medical doctors—including non-believers—determine whether the sick have experienced complete healing after visiting the shrine.

Of the four million visitors each year—in addition to the many millions who have visited since the mid-1800s when the miracles first began happening—only about seventy cases have been affirmed as miraculous healings.

When considering these rare cases at Lourdes, it is evident that God usually does not bypass the realities of the physical world. Even so, through the miracles that have taken place at the shrine, we have witnessed times when God has chosen to override laws of the physical world. Through these miracles, we see God's loving presence proclaimed through the Mother of the God-man, Jesus. Despite these miraculous healings, however, sickness, suffering, and death remain natural, normal consequences of living in this physical world.

Beyond the physical realm, human suffering also can come from personality differences in relationships. Two people who both want control can cause each other serious suffering if they do not handle their differences in a rational way. Emotional illness and behaviors that sometimes result from it—like addiction to alcohol—can lead to serious conflict in family relationships. All the challenges and weaknesses that come along with living in a physical world need intelligent prevention and intervention. By working through human instruments—whether they are professionals or people simply putting "love your neighbor" into practice—God provides light and strength through his grace, bringing intelligent prevention and intervention to situations where they are most needed.

Second Cause: Human Freedom Capable of Evil

For the most part, people treat each other with respect and practice the "love your neighbor as yourself" dictum. This innate goodness is present because each individual is made in God's own loving image and likeness. But each individual also possesses the freedom of the human will, and with that freedom also comes the power to choose good or evil.

There was a man in the Midwest who directed his evil energy toward a place that was dedicated to spiritual retreat. Before the retreat center was built in the woods, the man chose to buy property next to it. He then began spreading lies throughout the community about the intended use of the retreat property. "It will house criminals who will endanger our neighborhood," he told them. At the county planning office, he challenged construction of the retreat building. As a result of this man's lies and innuendo, the project experienced major delays. The retreat owner experienced a lot of concern and heartache when thinking about having to continue dealing with this neighbor's immoral behavior.

But God turns evil—like greed, meanness, and the ill-motivated desire to control others—to good end. The building contractor of the retreat center was a man of simple honesty and integrity. Never had he experienced anything like this man's behavior. But with intelligence and a calm demeanor, the building contractor countered every effort to sabotage the project at the county planning level. One of the new buildings, which had experienced construction delays, became a beautiful chapel by default—and much earlier than the retreat owner had planned. In this situation, as in many others, evil was brought to an unintended better end. The perpetrator of the evil behavior moved on, but he remained in the prayers of the retreat personnel. God's love and power remain ever-present and available.

Servanthood as Solution

In the face of sickness, suffering, and death—and also in man's personal capacity for evil—there are solutions. As illustrated in the previous story, those on the receiving end of the neighbor's evil behavior found a solution to the problem by trusting in God's loving servanthood. They continued to counter the evil behaviors with intelligence, while remembering their primary role as servants to future retreatants who needed the facility. As a result, county officials were able to hear and receive the truth about the situation. Truth won out. Servanthood—wishing good for all—also prevailed.

We can see in Scripture how Jesus handled unavoidable sickness, suffering, and death by practicing and modeling servanthood. Jesus did not want to suffer punishment and death, which he knew he would have to face as a result of the Pharisees' decision: "Abba, Father, all things are possible to you. Take this cup away from me…" (Mark 14:36). The powerful religious leaders had the authority to pursue Jesus' death. Jesus knew only a miracle could save him, and he acknowledged the Father could achieve this by sending angels. "But not what I will but what you will" (Mark 14:36). But based on the odds illustrated in our earlier discussion of Lourdes, miracles usually do not seem to play much of a part in God's plan. And in facing his own death and suffering, Jesus had to deal with that reality. As a servant of God, Jesus accepted the will of the Master—whether to allow the Pharisees' decision to stand or to deliver Jesus from the Pharisees' evil intent through a miracle. But the God-man experienced human suffering and dying on the cross at the hands of men with evil intent.

When others face sickness, suffering, or death, our servanthood becomes all the more important. In practicing servanthood toward others who face these difficult circumstances, we have one of the greatest opportunities to listen and respond to their needs. Caring for others who need our help is the greatest opportunity we have to practice servanthood. In fact, many nuns and religious orders have hospital ministry as their primary focus. Our recently beatified Mother Teresa served the helpless of Calcutta. But everyone in every family eventually faces sickness, suffering, and death over the years—often beginning with the care of a sick baby or child.

We Forgive God and Others

Blaming God for sickness, suffering, and death may seem to make sense. After all, logic seems to suggest that God causes all sickness, suffering, and death. And since God created the world and placed us in it, there's also the thought that God can prevent the bad things that happen to us. But as we have observed in some of the previous examples, the natural order of the physical world—along with man's capacity to choose evil—causes the majority of the bad circumstances we experience in this life. Nevertheless, we have a tendency to blame God. As a result, we may need to forgive God for wrongly attributing painful circumstances to him.

A good start in forgiving God lies in intelligently accepting the fact that God is not deliberately trying to hurt us. Physical realities and human evil create the majority of our suffering. Even so, all of us may sometimes ask God: "Why is this happening?" The nature of the physical world and the human capacity for evil are two logical answers. And while they are accurate, those two answers do not provide much comfort. In the end, we need to simply abandon ourselves—or a sick relative or friend—into God's loving care with simple childlike trust.

We may sometimes experience anger when dealing with sickness, suffering, or death in our lives. Through negligence, weakness, or evil intent, people sometimes create these conditions for themselves. Forgiving others for their part in causing sickness, suffering, or death also can be a real challenge. But we can look to Scripture for guidance. Both Mary and Jesus practiced the basic behavior of forgiveness by first asking, "Why?" Mary asked Jesus, "Why have you done this to us?"

when he abandoned them at age twelve (Luke 2:41–51). When Jesus was on the cross, he asked his Father: "My God, my God, why have you forsaken me?" (Matthew 27:46). In these examples, we observe Jesus and Mary asking "Why?" as a way to better understand situations that are painful.

We also can ask "Why?" when faced with difficult, painful circumstances. In answering that question, we may come to understand that those who hurt us did not know what they were doing or they decided to act on evil intent for their own benefit. In asking this question, we may arrive at some difficult, hard-to-accept answers. For example, we may find out the driver who ran a red light and smashed into our car was talking on a cell phone at the time of the accident. Or we might discover that the coworker who came to work with an infectious fever passed it to us and others.

No matter how much someone may have contributed to our sickness, suffering, or even death, the forgiveness behavior that Jesus emphasizes is demonstrated in the parable of the Prodigal Son (Luke 15:11–32). In the parable, the father wastes no time struggling to forgive the profligate son who had besmirched the family name. Instead, he threw a big party to welcome his son back home. Reaching out to those who harm us with the desire and effort to rebuild our loving relationship makes the most logical sense from a theological and spiritual perspective.

Jesus stated that the foundation of his entire message rests on the principle of loving God and our neighbor as we love ourselves. When someone hurts us, they harm that love relationship. But when we respond to hurtful behavior by reaching out in a positive way, we rebuild the relationship and bring it back to the way God wants all human relationships to be, now and for all eternity. From a psychological standpoint, responding in this way allows us to waste less energy thinking and worrying about the hurtful behavior. And when we respond to hurtful behavior with forgiveness, we often see the other person responding in a positive way.

Dealing Intelligently

With the intelligence God gives each of us, we assume major responsibility for avoiding sickness, suffering, and death, and for dealing with the unavoidable when these circumstances come our way. When Tony, our perfectly healthy six-month-old son, began convulsing in his crib late one night, we rushed him to Saint Joseph's Hospital emergency room and to the attached Barrow's Neurological Institute. A circle of doctors discussed and tended to the convulsion that lasted six hours and left Tony, who now is in his forties, functioning at no greater capacity than a three-year-old. His care has required years of difficult but accurate decisions. He is an emotionally healthy and sociable person—a product of continuous, intelligent, and loving care from many people. "What would be best for Tony and his caregivers?" is one of the most effective questions that has guided those involved in his care.

God does not want those he loves to give up. We must be instruments of God's love, and always seek good. Yet it can be difficult to find good in situations involving sickness, suffering, and death. So we must always challenge these conditions with questions that seek to deal with what may become unavoidable. And when we finally reach those unavoidable circumstances, we must trust and abandon ourselves to God's care, and always ask for guidance about what else God would have us do.

Speaking Out for Help

A final responsibility requires us to speak out for help when facing sickness or suffering. In the case of serious illness, we may ask many people to pray for us. We also may ask for a second or third medical opinion. And in the case of suffering caused by evil intent or human weakness, we may have to speak out by seeking legal or other professional help to end the negative behavior.

We should never succumb to illogical and theologically absurd statements like, "God must want this suffering." Instead, we must speak the truth and act on it. And what we know to be true is this:

"God loves us." We must listen to our own needs and the needs of others, and speak out to let others know the truth.

Feelings We Face

When facing sickness, suffering, and death, fear and concern affect all of us. When confronting sickness and suffering, it also is normal to experience many of the same feelings people have when facing death. In her books, Elisabeth Kübler-Ross—well-known psychiatrist and author—lists many feelings people often experience when facing death and other losses associated with sickness and suffering. Some of these feelings include denial, anger, bargaining with God, depression, grief, acceptance—and eventually, peace.

In my own experience, I experienced some denial in dealing with my diabetes. I then experienced a range of other emotions as I learned how to cope with the disease. Initially, I was upset that I had to deal with it, and I also experienced sadness and grief after the diagnosis. Eventually, I came to accept the daily medication, exercise, and the discipline of staying away from desserts as part of my life.

Other circumstances that people face in relationships and friendships can generate many of the same feelings people have when moving through the grief process described by Elisabeth Kübler-Ross in her books. For example, suffering the put-downs of a friend might take a person through some of the same feelings that accompany the grief process—denial, anger, depression, acceptance of unsuccessful attempts to stop the hurtful behavior, and peace after deciding to move on and invest in other friendships.

Connect With Jesus' Mysteries of Suffering and Death

Blessed Abbot Marmion offers powerful assistance for receiving special graces from God when dealing with sickness, suffering, and death. Declared Blessed in the year 2000, Marmion and his writings on this issue now have full backing from the Church. Basing his teachings on the writings of Saint Paul, Marmion describes special "reservoirs of grace" that Jesus, the God-man, created through his own human actions. For example, when Jesus suffered in the Garden as he reflected on his impending death, he created for us a special reservoir of grace. We now are able to draw from this reservoir when we face difficult situations and suffering in our own lives.

We can access these special graces and aid our intellect in dealing with suffering in our own lives by putting the following behaviors into practice:

✴ Recall a situation in Jesus' life similar to the situation you now face—particularly those involving sickness, suffering, or death.

✴ Have faith in the special graces that Jesus obtained for you by dealing with a situation similar to yours. Through these special graces, you can find the strength to handle the situation you face in your own life.

✴ Reach out in love and thanksgiving to Jesus for his special assistance.

✴ Trust in these special graces from God to successfully handle what comes your way when thinking through and acting on decisions in your own situation.

Through God's special graces, we receive the gifts of accurate judgment, intelligence, and the strength of will to follow through on what we face in our own lives.

Exercise: Deal With Sickness and Suffering Ahead of Time

It is possible to make decisions about situations before they happen in our lives. The questions below offer some examples of how we can prepare to deal with future sickness and suffering in our own lives and in the lives of others. Dealing with death also can be included as part of the group discussion after doing this exercise with adults.

Deciding whether to talk to younger family members about facing death should be left to the discretion of adults. Having this discussion with children younger than six or seven generally is not recommended.

What emotions and thoughts have I experienced during past illnesses? How would I like to deal with future serious illness that I may have to face or that my loved ones may have to face?

How will I behave toward someone who says mean things to me or to others about me? What are some other situations that might cause hurt or suffering in my life? How do I want to handle those situations?

How do I want to face my own death, knowing that I might have to face it at some point in the future, or as early as tomorrow or *today*? How would I handle a serious illness like inoperable cancer? How do I want to deal with the gradual loss of health and quality of life in my old age?

Chapter Nine

Good News for Singles and the Chaste

James is divorced and single. But having a relationship—along with emotional and physical intimacy—are important to him. Even sharing the day's happenings with a beloved partner seems to fit the Genesis dictum, "It is not good for the man to be alone. I will make a suitable partner for him" (Genesis 2:18). Given what he values in life, James wonders: "Should I look for another wife?" General dissatisfaction and the feeling that marriage should provide a more perfect compatibility led to James' divorce. Even so, James sometimes wonders whether he expected too much of marriage. The nation's high divorce rate—around fifty percent—suggests that many people may have similar mixed feelings about marriage. Statistics also show that about sixty percent of second marriages end in divorce. Given all these statistics, what is the truth about the value of being single?

Life Without a Marriage Partner

Many people live without a marriage partner—divorced singles, young adult singles, widows, priests, and Sisters and Brothers who belong to religious orders. Others who are single often include Catholic couples who are engaged singles—with fifty percent of those living together, a percentage that also matches the general population statistic. Are unmarried people generally happy with their life situation? Many might counter this inquiry by asking the same question of married couples. Can one survive—and be happy—without a marriage partner?

Based on the increasing size of the human population, it appears that people are fairly successful when it comes to relationships. It also appears that many have the need to make those relationships with a loved one permanent. This need seems to align with feelings that often accompany a love relationship: "This is the only one for me. This will last forever." In fact, marriage ceremonies in the United States still include the phrase, "Until death parts us." Most marriage partners want full sexual union with their loved one, and they want those relationships to be permanent. And while the fruit of sexual union tends to happen naturally, the desire for permanency in a marriage is not accomplished as easily.

For most people, marriage seems to be the logical, natural way to meet the need for physical and emotional intimacy. But is a satisfying human relationship only possible in marriage? No. Nuns provide proof to the contrary with their active love relationship with God, as do priests, widows, and young adults with their chaste friendships. However, the unmet need for human relationship can create great unhappiness.

The God-Given Centrality of Human Relationship

The need for human relationship is part of the fundamental message that God brought to earth through Jesus. "You shall love the Lord, your God, with all your heart, and with all your soul, and with all your mind…You shall love your neighbor as yourself" (Matthew 22:37–39).

To love someone is to do good for that person and to share talents with that person (Matthew 25:14–30). God made us in his own image to be loving toward others. Sharing compatible talents or skills with one's entire mind and soul is the essence of a strong friendship. This kind of friendship also describes our future eternal life with God and others. The enjoyment and richness that result from sharing compatible personalities and skills is a gift from God, who intends for love to be central to our existence, now and forever.

In practice, relationships with relatives often can provide this kind of friendship. However, enjoyable friendships often are found outside the family—and hopefully sooner rather than later in life. Friendship also can be found in the careful and astute choice of a marriage partner. Understanding one's own skills, and staying alert to those same skills in others as described in previous chapters, also can help the single person make good friendship choices.

Another issue concerns homosexual and lesbian friendships. Years ago, while conducting individual counseling sessions about conflict in some of these relationships, I asked some of these clients to describe the emotional progression of their love relationship from the beginning to the present. In describing their relationships, I realized that the progression they described coincided with the emotional progression of my own heterosexual relationships. My own experience of friendship with those who are gay—whether friends, relatives, lay people, or religious—has been comfortable and enriching.

Emotional Illness Without Human Relationship

Before exploring the impact of not having an enjoyable relationship in one's life, we need to explore the term *human relationship*. Two people of either gender can have an enjoyable friendship. As part of this friendship, they talk or communicate with each other regularly—in person, over the phone, or via the Internet. When spending time together, they enjoy each other's company. They may well admire the qualities of the other person, while also choosing to put up with weaknesses or differences in personality. But for the most part, two people who are friends simply enjoy communicating and spending time together. Generally, enjoying spending time with the other person comes from sharing one or more compatible personality traits and skills as described in Chapter Two.

Digressing for a moment from the discussion about single individuals, let's take a moment to look inside some marriage relationships that are not enjoyable friendships. In my years of private-practice counseling, I experienced how terrible a marriage relationship can be. In counseling sessions with many married couples, I witnessed irrational anger, anxiety, and depression at its worst. Many of these conditions existed due to years of personality conflict and emotional illness that often resulted. In most of these situations, the couples involved had not succeeded in listening to and accepting each other's strong, but different, personality needs. Both partners wanted different things out of life. In many cases, just being in the other partner's presence irritated them. Emotional and physical violence also were present in some of the cases.

Among priests and religious Sisters and Brothers, we also find some who experience serious anxiety, addictions, and other symptoms of emotional illness. Some of these are the result of a misguided concept of celibacy that includes beliefs like: "No enjoyable friendship is safe if you are celibate." Carrying that idea around as one's first principle of human relationship, it is easy to understand how a celibate person can fall into an irrational misunderstanding of how God made us. The repercussions that result from not accepting the God-given need for personal human relationships are perilous. People also can get into trouble with thoughts like, "All these feelings of strong emotional attraction or sexual yearnings are terrible." These thoughts and beliefs, and others like them, can be emotionally harmful to young adults, widows, and other singles who are striving to live a chaste life.

Error of the "Third Way" for Religious and Others

Another major caveat regarding strong friendships rests in what is known as the "Third Way," which still is practiced by some in today's celibate culture. It involves a strong friendship in which the celibate surrenders to the falling-in-love experience—to the point of an exclusive emotional relationship with all the demands that entails—even though the other person may be another celibacy-vowed individual, a single lay person, or even someone who is married. Such a relationship may not include sexual behavior, but it may exhibit all the exclusivity and emotional closeness short of that type of union.

According to a superior general of a major international religious order, this practice of anti-celibacy strong friendship began among priests and religious in the 1960s and 1970s. Father Pedro Arrupe, the former Jesuit superior general, condemned this behavior during his tenure from 1969 to 1983. Other Jesuit writers referred to this phenomenon as "having your cake and eating it, too."

Third Way behavior remains a contradiction to the commitment of celibacy. The emotional closeness and bonding in a romantic relationship between the sexes was intended by God as a pathway to the full sexual expression of becoming "two in one flesh." By contrast, celibacy demands commitment to an exclusive body-and-soul love relationship with God. The progression of this Third Way behavior and emotional mind-set can easily lead to the abandonment of one's celibate vocation by good-willed people as they struggle with the il-logic of this contradictory way of life.

This same exclusive and emotional love connection from falling in love also can lead to divorce and remarriage among married individuals. I would state again that this God-created emotional experience simply comes from a compatibility of talents. Even though it feels like one has to follow through when these feelings are experienced, it absolutely is not necessary. The proper course of action must come from reason, followed by the prayer-supported strength to follow through with that decision.

The Four Solutions Applied to Single Life

How can the four-solution behaviors Jesus practiced help those in the single life? Servanthood can include listening to one's own legitimate needs, such as the need for compatible, enjoyable human friendship. Acting as an instrument of God toward oneself, the single person must aggressively pursue finding and growing these kinds of friendships. One also can focus on renewing old friendships with relatives, former coworkers, and others. Church associations such as Saint Vincent de

Paul or Bible study groups also can provide a number of opportunities for finding and establishing new friendships. In searching for friendships, it is helpful to remember that listening and responding to the needs of others is servanthood behavior that makes us a desirable friend.

The practice of forgiveness also may help those who are single. In some cases, we may need to forgive God if we have not yet found a truly compatible, enjoyable relationship, marriage partner, or friend. Or we may need to forgive and stop blaming our experience of hurtful loneliness on the friend or marriage partner who left us. A single person may be left out of the kind of socializing that married couples enjoy with others who are married. Getting to the "why" of these and other hurts helps us to understand, and ultimately, to let go of them. Reaching out in positive ways toward those who have hurt us also can be helpful.

When major personal needs surface in the life of a single person, the most immediate solution lies in the use of the intellect. Ask questions that help identify the need. "Do I need a compatible, enjoyable, ongoing friendship?" "Do I need to know if this person or that person is truly compatible with me?" "Do I need to reenvision what I want to do with my life?" "Do I need to discern if I have chosen my life as a religious because I personally wanted it (which can be a distinct sign of vocational grace) or because it seemed better at the time than another alternative (and therefore might not be the grace of a Spirit-led vocation)?"

These and many other need-to-deal-with questions can jump-start others that can lead to intelligent and well-discerned decisions, as well as peaceful actions.

Sometimes single people without close friends must rely upon themselves to get their needs met. The starting point for attending to one's own needs again begins with asking questions. "What legitimate need of mine is not being met?" "What would meet this need?" "What are some alternatives if that does not work?" "Who can help me with this issue?"

Then the single person must decide how to speak out effectively in pursuing this need and with whom. A frequent question from ecclesial ministers who attend my seminars is: "How can I make headway on an issue with someone who will not listen to me?" I suggested asking this question, as one possibility: "Who already has a good relationship with this person, and can I direct my concerns and suggestions toward that person?"

What Kind of Relationship Works for the Single Life?

The typical description of a marital relationship involves strong personality attraction, the experience of falling in love, a fruitful sexual union that results in children, and a strong bond between both partners. Cohabiting engaged couples, religious and others involved in a Third Way relationship, as well as other ways of pursuing the emotional exclusivity of married life remain a concern as we examine how singles can achieve lives of loving friendship.

We have established the legitimacy and theological necessity of loving friendships. For Catholics, marriage provides a sacrament for those involved in a wholly complete and loving relationship. What human relationship is available to singles that is legitimate and has the ability to meet the needs and goals of the single person? The term legitimate in this context does not include a discussion of sexual, emotionally binding, and exclusive relationship. It does, however, include compatibility of personality and skills, enjoyment of another's company, conversation, long-term friendships, and support.

Legitimate friendship provides enjoyment that comes from a natural feeling that God intends for all humans. Some friendships provide more natural enjoyment than others as a result of greater compatibility in personal strengths, as described in earlier chapters. And hopefully, those who want a marriage relationship will use patient and wise judgment in the choice of a partner so that there is natural compatibility between both individuals.

Sometimes a married individual may find a more compatible friendship with a single person—especially later in life. In such cases, however, these must remain non-sexual, non-emotionally charged friendships. Emotional exclusivity must remain a hallmark of the marriage relationship. In these situations, one must avoid acting on the temptation to change relationships. It is important in these situations to remember that the feeling of falling in love usually comes with a God-given natural desire for exclusivity. However, this instinct can be ignored without psychological harm. Patient emotional, and even physical, separation will prove how ignoring such feelings can give one freedom from them.

In conclusion, a friendship that works and is legitimate for a single or celibate person includes:

✳ Enjoying spending time with a friend who has similar personality skills and traits (see Chapter Two).

✳ Ignoring feelings of falling in love that can be triggered by one or more compatible personality skills.

✳ Enjoying friendship within the bounds dictated by reason and an informed conscience.

Special Appeal to Priests and Religious as Celibate Singles

As suggested throughout this chapter, all God's children are expected to enjoy loving friendships. Servanthood—or listening and responding to the needs of others—provides a spirituality behavior that was modeled by Jesus and that can be followed by everyone. Servanthood describes the essence of love, including the rational pursuit of the loved one's good. In servanthood lies the key to loving behavior toward others.

Priests and religious should not fear strong friendships, even though compatibility may trigger feelings of falling in love. When these feelings arise, they do not require action. For example, these feelings do not mean in the words of one pastor, "If I fall in love, I will immediately leave the priesthood to be with her and remain honest to that love." This type of declaration does not fit with reality. The experience of falling in love is a God-given natural phenomenon. But God also has given us the intelligence to balance all of our feelings with reason. In the present structure of the Roman Catholic Church, priests and religious freely accept celibacy as a required part of the priesthood or religious life during the discernment process for their vocation. Falling in love is a challenge to that calling, but not an insurmountable one. The experience of falling in love remains a natural, God-given part of the human makeup that can be both ignored and appreciated.

My appeal to priests and religious is to keep your celibacy intact. The beauty of your sacrifice provides not only great grace for you, but also for all members of the mystical body. I understand that your vow or promise (for diocesan priests) of celibacy confers no special graces other than the normal graces of chastity that everyone receives. But those latter graces assist the intellect in making correct moral judgments and provide the strength to carry them out. Dealing correctly with the falling-in-love experience can be achieved with practical help from God.

My appeal regarding the friendships of priests and religious also extends to their parishioners and relatives. Aggressively develop friendships with one or more priests and religious whose company you enjoy. Invite them for a meal. Get to know their thoughts and feelings on issues of interest to both of you. Go out of your way to develop an enjoyable and legitimate friendship that God wants them to have as well.

Exercise: Eliminate Loneliness

Feelings of loneliness can be expected as part of a single person's life. Being single means being alone. However, being with someone else does not guarantee the absence of loneliness. Some married partners describe their marital relationship as lonely. I have provided the following exercise in seminars to both single and married individuals, as it helps eliminate the feeling of loneliness. It works as follows:

Recall at least one occasion or relationship that caused or now causes you to feel lonely. Concentrate on that feeling of loneliness when recalling that situation.

Recall at least one occasion when a person or people you were with made you feel special. For example, they may have praised you for who you are or something that you did. Or think of an accomplishment that still makes you feel good about yourself.

Notice how your feeling of loneliness has disappeared.

The obvious lesson from this exercise is that feeling worthwhile directly contradicts and eliminates the feelings of loneliness. You may have to repeat this exercise to rid yourself of the feeling. But each time you do the exercise, you teach your emotional memory a truth that contradicts loneliness: "I am worthwhile just for who I am."

Chapter Ten

The Mass:
Light and Strength for Our Daily Problems

My own daily work problems often involve resolving multiple issues related to writing a book. Do I need an opening story summarizing the chapter's message? Or, in reflecting on this final chapter, I wondered, "How can I help people connect the obvious value of the Mass to solving their daily problems?" After many years of dealing with such work challenges, I stumbled across the following definition: Grace is a special gift from God that provides light for our intellect and strength for our will. It allows us to arrive at and follow through with the right judgments and decisions. Grace is exactly what I needed to solve my writing problems. And as Mass is defined as our primary source of grace, I began attending Mass more often during the weekdays. In looking back over my written work, I began to see that the times when I was stuck were also the times when my own skills were not enough to get me unstuck on their own. I soon realized that God's Holy Spirit was the source of the breakthrough help I always needed to get unstuck.

Weekly Mass seems a reasonable practice for concerned Catholics who want all the help they can get in dealing with challenges in their work and family lives. Solving daily issues around marriage, parenting, the single life, and suffering in its many forms requires intelligent resolution and strong follow-through. Through focused attendance at Mass, God's grace promises help with these challenges.

To be effective, focused attendance at Mass is needed. For example, if we are unaware that our child or a friend needs help, nothing will happen. Similarly, if we are not fully present throughout the Mass, the potential for the liturgy to help us is negligible. The Mass is not magical. It requires our conscious and active participation. As you may have noticed in a friend or relative, one can attend Mass and yet experience no change in one's behaviors or attitudes. Yet the freely God-given gifts of grace are designed to make us more like God in our attitudes and in behaviors like servanthood and forgiveness. Without question, change takes time. But change happens when we consciously seek the God-given power of grace.

Why We Need Help and How to Get It

Every day provides ample evidence that we need help in dealing with challenges in our family and work lives. Our relationships—whether with a marriage partner, relative, friend, or coworker—provide the potential for daily challenges. These people each have different and new needs like we do. Daily challenges also can come from circumstances like sickness, the workplace, from the weather, and even from mechanical problems. Each challenge or situation requires us to make various judgments and decisions. Sometimes, just recalling daily demands is enough to exhaust a person.

Dealing with each situation requires intelligent judgment, insight into the relevant facts, awareness of our own needs and the needs of others. Some situations may require moral judgments, as well as guidance from our conscience. Our final decisions are then based on all the facts that we have gathered in each situation. Our ability to discern and arrive at the truth, as well as the ability to discover the right solution for each situation, comes from the powerful intelligence of our soul. Even so, our human intellect has its limits. There is not a person alive today who always comes up with a perfect, workable solution to every problem. Even Jesus was challenged at Cana when his mother insisted that the time to start his ministry had arrived. This was contrary to Jesus' own judgment: "My hour has not yet come" (John 2:1–11). But Jesus respected Mary's judgment and changed the water into wine.

Even when we arrive at a workable solution to a problem, a major hurdle still remains: Will we follow through? As Saint Paul says, "For I do not what I want, but I do what I hate" (Romans 7:15). Obstacles to acting on our well-thought-out solutions can come from many sources. In some cases, others will resist our judgment. Or we may lack the emotional energy to bring about the change. Other obstacles like procrastination, laziness, cowardice, lack of caring, questioning our judgment, and general confusion also can get in our way.

How can we get the help we need to make the right judgments and decisions when handling situations and following through on them? First of all, God gave us the powers of intellect and will to apply to our daily problems. These two gifts—knowing and loving—reflect the essence of divinity and God's power. In this way, God gave us the skills we need to deal with our life on earth. This same intellect and will, along with grace, also make it possible to enter into a personal love relationship with God and with each other for all eternity. The gift of sanctifying grace that begins with our baptism allows us to fully participate in a life and relationship with God.

God helps our intellect and will function beyond what is humanly possible, with the sanctifying, actual, and sacramental graces he makes available to us every day. We have to cooperate with those graces to receive them, and this involves seeking them out in our daily prayer and in the sacraments. "Give us each day our daily bread" (Luke 11:3) encompasses all of our daily needs—including help from God's supernatural, all-powerful grace, which is available to us in dealing with all of life's situations.

Sometimes, the intellect can produce errors in judgment when trying to identify solutions to various problems. Procrastination and other human weaknesses also can hamper the follow-through of our will. Grace provides us with special gifts that can increase with time—gifts like wisdom, wise counsel, fortitude, and temperance to assist our natural will. God's graces also help us resolve the daily, specific problems that require our intellect and problem-solving skills. All of these gifts—along with special sacramental graces that include growth in our personal relationship with Christ through the Eucharist—give us the assistance we need beyond our limited human skills. To fully access these gifts requires humility. A lack of humility about the limitations inherent in our human intellect can contribute to our frailty.

Planning Ahead for the Light and Strength

You may hear parishioners complain that they get nothing out of Mass or the homily. A lack of attention or focus during Mass contributes to that negative experience, and we will deal at length with how to resolve that problem. Planning ahead also is needed to access the most help from Mass for our daily lives.

Planning ahead for Mass can be accomplished by simply reflecting on and discussing the three Scripture readings for the upcoming Sunday Mass with family members. Many parishes simply list the readings on a website or in a bulletin so you can look them up in your own copy of the Old and New Testaments. Other parishes supply the full text for each reading on their websites, allowing families to print off copies for each member. The entire text of the readings also can be found by "Googling" websites like the one for United States Conference of Catholic Bishops. Under a tab on the main page called "Readings," people can access the readings and psalms for each day of the month from *the New American Bible.* How to incorporate these readings into the weekly routine depends on individual preference. Some may prefer reflecting on the readings alone, while others may enjoy discussing them with family members, or with one or more friends. "What did you get out of the reading?" is a good, legitimate question for everyone to ask following each reading.

In the next two sections of this chapter, we will explore *Lectio Divina* and the Mysteries as two powerful ways of drawing conscious and unconscious graces from each of the readings. We also will apply these readings to the situations we face in our own lives. In fact, the Church now states that every priest should connect these readings to parishioners' daily lives in each homily.

Journaling in a notebook or writing your thoughts on a file card as you follow the *Lectio Divina* and Mysteries exercises will help you get the most out of the readings. You can then review your notes before or on the way to Mass, and also recall your personal insights at the appropriate times during Mass.

Lectio Divina: Direct Conversation with God from the Readings

Lectio Divina, which means divine reading, is one of the most ancient and accepted approaches to talking with God in the sacred Scriptures. It also gives us a powerful way to experience each of the Sunday readings.

While reading through the Old Testament (one reading), and the New Testament (one epistle reading, and one Gospel reading), underline or circle any word, phrase, sentence that strikes you as different or special. The experience of noticing key words or phrases in Scripture can be God communicating with you.

In response, ask yourself, "What might God be telling me based on what I have underlined?" The answer to your question may be God speaking to you through your intellect—even though you will only experience it as your own thinking, not as a voice directly from God.

Then ask yourself, "What will I do in response to what God may be telling me?" In this way, God's grace can direct you toward a behavior change for the good, and help you to become more like Christ.

Turn the "What I will do?" graced answer of your intellect into a prayer of petition. In your prayer, ask God to help you follow through on doing that more Christlike behavior revealed to you while reading Scripture.

After years of using this practice—with everyone from young children to senior citizens—the majority describe unique conclusions from a word they found most interesting in Scripture. Often, it is the same word that spoke to others while doing the same exercise.

But the similarity of experience stops there. While people may focus on the same word, each person has a different perspective when they consider what it means to them, what God might be saying to them, and what kind of behavior they need to do in response. This unique individual experience often indicates that grace is present, and that God is in conversation with each person. I believe these experiences demonstrate how much God wants to communicate with us. If lack of interest, lack of concentration, or other factors interfere with this process, simply try again at a later time.

The Mysteries of Jesus: Specific Help for Our Life from the Readings

Based on the recent beatification of Blessed Abbot Columba Marmion, OSB, his "mysteries of Jesus" have become an acceptable application of Saint Paul's theology so that we can gain the help and guidance we need by studying the life of Jesus. Since Jesus was the God-man, each act of Jesus created what Marmion calls unique "reservoirs of grace." We can draw on these reservoirs to assist our intellect and to deal with similar situations in our own lives.

You can use the following process to draw on the power from the "mysteries of Jesus":

In this Sunday's Gospel reading, look for situations in Jesus' words or behaviors that reflect similar circumstances in your own life that are currently creating problems, conflict, or stress.

Reach out in faith by praying: "Jesus, I believe that as God-man you made available for me the special graces to handle this situation as you handled yours."

Reach out in love by saying something like: "Jesus, I love you and thank you for your power to help me in this situation."

In doing the *Lectio Divina* and the Mysteries of Jesus exercises and applying them to the three readings for each Sunday's Mass, we receive strong graces from God to assist us in solving problems and making necessary changes in behavior and attitude to deal with our current life situations. These graces also are quietly and gradually changing us into the person God wants us to be by making us more effective in dealing with our problems. Doing these exercises also better prepares us to receive the wisdom and strength we need from the Sunday Mass to help deal with those same situations and problems. Maintaining the right focus during the Mass also is an important factor in accessing God's help with the situations and problems we face in our daily lives.

Staying Focused in Mass to Receive the Most Powerful Help

Staying focused and conscious during Mass is key to accessing its most powerful help. The Liturgy of the Word and the Liturgy of the Eucharist are the two main parts of the Mass. During the Liturgy of the Word, we actively concentrate on the three readings we focused on in our private reflections or family discussions, and while doing the *Lectio Divina* and the Mysteries exercises. While sitting in Mass and as we listen to the readings or homily, we may hear new words or phrases—other than the ones we focused on during *Lectio Divina*—that capture our attention. Upon hearing new words or phrases that speak to us, we can quickly do a new *Lectio Divina* or Mysteries reflection and apply the insight we receive to the situations we encounter in our daily lives. By gradually developing this skill, we can find *one word*—even in a poorly presented homily—that, thanks to God's grace, can still provide an answer to a problem we are facing in our daily life.

In the Liturgy of the Eucharist, there are two major events to focus on and actively participate in during Mass. We are called to offer ourselves with Jesus at the same time that the priest offers up to God the sacrifice of Jesus—who is fully present on the altar in the external appearance of bread and wine. We do this in unity with the entire congregation. This part of the Mass also is meaningful to me because of the connection through prayer with those who have already gone to heaven.

Secondly, we go to receive that same Jesus in holy Communion. This time of focus normally provides the most consciously intimate and special personal time during the Mass. During this time, we can easily talk to the God-man who has approached us in love with a desire to be of help. To do this, we must extend ourselves consciously to Jesus in love, thanksgiving, and petition for our needs and for the needs of others. Fascinating to me is the fact that our Church teaches us that this sacrament offers unique, special graces that allows us to recommit ourselves to the poor. What could be more Christlike than that?

Recently I had the joy of coming across a book called *The Ministry of the Assembly* by Caroline M. Thomas. The author provides several ways of consciously focusing on and staying active in each part of the Mass. I recommend purchasing this short book. With increasing focus, each individual and family can experience powerful graces throughout Mass that can help meet the challenges of daily life.

Family Testimonies to the Power of the Mass

There is no greater proof of the power of Mass than testimonies from couples with multiple children who have firsthand experience with that power in their daily family and work lives. I first listened to more than two hours of testimony from a young couple with five children, including a fourteen-year-old. At least one parent—and at times the whole family—attends daily Mass. I also listened to testimony from an older couple with three children, ranging in age from sixteen to twenty-three. In twenty-six years of marriage, they have never missed a Sunday Mass with their children.

My question was: "What proof do you have that the Mass helped you deal with your family and work situations?" In my twenty-five years of counseling that involved multiple family and work issues, I have never heard family experiences where more grace was present than I heard in more than four hours I spent with both of these families.

I walked away with many of their observations and reflections, which I will share here in summary and through a few of their actual quotes. The younger couple told me they find Mass to be a protection against the anxieties of daily life. It puts God in the center of their day with the "added grace in making decisions and having patience." By making this commitment to go to Mass, they have experienced a growing dependence on God, trusting that "God will feed us." "It slows my crazy life down, even for the thirty-minute period." "It forces me to look at the way I deal with my children and my spouse." "Mass gives me an understanding of the big picture, not just my immediate life, but the eternal." "It has greatly increased the power of my conscience. At work, it gives me the strength to stand up for what is right versus how the business world is." "We as a whole family are just more graced toward each other." "Mass is just like exercise. You know it is having an effect as you keep doing it."

Their fourteen-year-old responded to the same question from his mom with: "Mass helps me start the day on a positive note. It is an OK day if no Mass, but a great day with it. Homilies have helped me back up my faith when someone challenged me."

After years of attending weekly Mass, one of the partners in the older couple put it this way: "Mass is a weekly meeting between God and us, just like at the office's weekly board meeting."

"The Mass gives us so many opportunities, like to reflect on what we have done and a place where we can ask for God's continued guidance." "We can thank God there for things we take for granted and should be thankful for."

For this couple, weekly Mass provided them with the opportunity to show their children the importance of consistency and the values that are important in life. Now, they see their adult children still devoted to the Church. Even though friends tell this couple how lucky they are, they pointed out that their children's devotedness to the Mass came from hard work, starting when their children were very little. The children were taught the importance of Mass, due in part to consistent attendance and also to parental teachings. "This is God's house, like when we go to grandma and grandpa's. It is a special time." "You are going to need help some day that we cannot give you. Only God will be able to. So you have to go to Mass even in the good times of your life, and God will help you in the bad times. Your efforts at Mass attendance will be worth it throughout your life."

Mass brings this couple "a sense of comfort, a peace of mind." "When we are faced with a hard decision, we ask God's help and we trust and know God will help." "Even when suddenly faced with the difficulty of replacing an employee, I learned you do not just ask for help when you need help, but you need to have a relationship with God all the time." "We have a confidence in God that we did not have in our first years of marriage. But we promised each other on our wedding day that we would commit to weekly Mass."

In a major surgery event a few years ago, "I never felt such calmness and peace. I had no doubt it was coming from my relationship with God. I had learned to talk to him as my best friend. I have built this relationship with God over time, though at first going to Mass was just going through the motions." "Primarily, just go to Mass. It doesn't happen overnight. It takes time to experience the effects."

My overall observation about these two couples was the unusual peace and comfort they had with each other, with their children, and with the world around them—in spite of all of life's difficulties and challenges. They also exhibited the excellent judgment and follow-through that are the hallmarks of graced lives. They possessed no pretense, and no pride. God was clearly forming them into the best they could be. These couples also demonstrated a primary allegiance to God, with weekly Mass at the center of their lives. Their commitment to the value of the Mass in their lives clearly has empowered them. And the Mass—with its daily life-changing graces is transforming them beyond what I would consider normal human development.

Exercise: Questions to Ask Yourself at Mass

Through its power, grace works on our soul, intellect, and will. Asking a question forces the intellect to search out an answer, and based on the facts gathered, find the truth in a situation. Our will gives us the power we need to follow through on solutions our intellect discovers so that we are able to deal with life's challenges. But grace also works in our intellect and will to help us become more like Christ and Mary, the most perfect of Christians. We open ourselves up to this grace by regularly attending and actively participating in Mass. We actively participate by bringing questions that are relevant to our current lives, as well as determination to follow through on the answers that come to us during Mass. These questions express some of the recommendations earlier in this chapter.

Choose at least one question for each Mass until you find one that is helpful to you. In addition, ask yourself what other question might help you stay focused during Mass.

1. *What action was revealed to me in my preparation for Mass during the* **Lectio Divina** *or the Mysteries exercises? Based on this insight, what is it that I want to ask God when I think about carrying out this action?*

2. *What help do I want to ask Jesus for during Mass?*

3. *What situations or concerns from my life this past week do I want to offer up as Jesus offers himself in sacrifice to the Father?*

4. *In thinking about a problem in my life, what special parts of the Mass are likely to offer the most help? The "confession" near the beginning? Help from the readings? The offering of my problem along with Jesus' offering? Asking Jesus for help with the problem during Communion?*

5. *What in my life this past week do I want to thank God for?*

6. *What help for the poor can I commit to when I receive Jesus in Communion?*

7. *Who do I want to pray for or talk to Jesus about during the Mass?*

Bibliography

These works were consulted in the preparation of this book or are recommended for further reading.

Ball, Ann. *A Handbook of Catholic Sacramentals.* Huntington, IN: Our Sunday Visitor Publishing Division, 1991.

Barbernitz, Patricia. *Parish Ministry for Returning Catholics.* Mahwah, NJ: Paulist Press, 1993.

Barry, William A., and William J. Connolly. *Finding God in All Things: A Companion to the Spiritual Exercises of St. Ignatius.* Notre Dame, IN: Ave Maria Press, 1991.

Bausch, William J. *The Total Parish Manual: Everything You Need to Empower Your Faith Community.* Mystic, CT: Twenty-Third Publications, 1994.

Brennan, Patrick. *The Way of Forgiveness: How to Heal Life's Hurts and Restore Broken Relationships.* Ann Arbor, MI: Servant Publications, 2000.

Brown, Raymond E. An *Introduction to New Testament Christology.* Mahwah, NJ: Paulist Press, 1994.

Brown, Richard C. A *Practical Guide for Starting an Adult Faith Formation Program.* San Jose, CA: Resource Publications, Inc., 2003.

Brown, Richard C. *When Ministry Is Messy: Practical Solutions to Difficult Problems.* Cincinnati, OH: Saint Anthony Messenger Press, 2006.

Buby, S. M., Bertrand. *Mary of Galilee: Mary in the New Testament, Vol. 1.* New York, NY: Alba House, 1994.

Burke, O.P., John. *A Good News Spirituality: Finding Holiness in Parish Life*. Mahwah, NJ: Paulist Press, 2000.

Campbell, Jim. *52 Simple Ways to Talk With Your Kids About Faith*. Chicago, IL: Loyola Press, 2007.

Carson, Lillian. *The Essential Grandparent: A Guide to Making a Difference*. Deerfield Beach, FL: Health Communications, Inc., 1996.

Chandler, Phyllis; Burney, Joan; Leatherman, Mary Kay. *Sharing the Faith with Your Child: From Birth to Age Four*. Liguori, MO: Liguori Publications, 2006.

Chittister, Joan D. *Heart of Flesh: A Feminist Spirituality for Women and Men*. Grand Rapids, MI: William B. Eerdmans Publishing Company, 1998.

Chittister, Joan D. *Scarred by Struggle, Transformed by Hope*. Grand Rapids, MI: William B. Eerdmans Publishing Company, 2003.

Ciarrocchi, Joseph W. *A Minister's Handbook of Mental Disorders*. Mahwah, NJ: Paulist Press, 1993.

Clark, Capuchin, Keith. *An Experience of Celibacy*. Notre Dame, IN: Ave Maria Press, 1982.

Comer, Ronald J. *Fundamentals of Abnormal Psychology*. New York, NY: Worth Publishers, 2002.

Connell, Martin, ed. *The Catechetical Documents: A Parish Resource*. Chicago, IL: Liturgy Training Publications, 1996.

Cozzens, Donald B. *The Changing Face of the Priesthood*. Collegeville, MN: The Liturgical Press, 2000.

Dolan, Jay P., and Allan Figueroa Deck, S.J. *Hispanic Catholic Culture in the U.S.* Notre Dame, IN: University of Notre Dame Press, 1994.

Fromm, Erich. *The Art of Loving*. New York, NY: Harper & Row, 1956.

Gillen, Marie A., and Maurice C. Taylor, editors. *Adult Religious Education: A Journey of Faith Development*. Mahwah, NJ: Paulist Press, 1995.

Gillespie, S.J., C. Kevin. *Psychology and American Catholicism*. New York, NY: The Crossroad Publishing Company, 2001.

Greeley, Andrew M. *The Catholic Revolution: New Wine, Old Wineskins, and the Second Vatican Council*. Berkeley, CA: University of California Press, 2002.

Greeley, Andrew M. *Priests: A Calling in Crisis.* Chicago, IL: The University of Chicago Press, 2004.

Green, S.J., Thomas H. *Come Down Zacchaeus: Spirituality & the Laity.* Notre Dame, IN: Ave Maria Press,1988.

Greenleaf, Robert (Larry Spears, ed.). *Servant Leadership: A Journey into the Nature of Legitimate Power & Greatness.* Mahwah, NJ: Paulist Press, 2002.

Groeschel, C.F.R., Benedict J. *The Courage to be Chaste.* Mahwah, NJ: Paulist Press, 1985.

Gula, Richard M. *Ethics in Pastoral Ministry.* Mahwah, NJ: Paulist Press, 1996.

Hart, Thomas N. *The Art of Christian Listening.* Mahwah, NJ: Paulist Press, 1980.

Hater, Reverend Robert J. *The Catholic Family in a Changing World.* Orlando, FL: Harcourt, 2005.

Hater, Reverend Robert J. *When a Catholic Marries a Non-Catholic.* Cincinnati, OH: Saint Anthony Messenger Press, 2006.

Johnson, Richard P. *A Christian's Guide to Mental Wellness.* Liguori, MO: Liguori Publications, 1990.

Johnston, William. *Mystical Theology: the Science of Love.* Maryknoll, NY: Orbis Books, 2000.

Kavanaugh, O.C.D., Kieran, and Otilio Rodriguez, O.C.D., translators. *The Collected Works of Saint John of the Cross.* Washington, D.C.: ICS Publications, Institute of Carmelite Studies, 1991.

Kavanaugh, O.C.D., Kieran, and Otilio Rodriguez, O.C.D., translators.. *The Collected Works of Saint Theresa of Avila*, Volume One. Washington, D.C.: ICS Publications, Institute of Carmelite Studies, 1987.

Kavanaugh, O.C.D., Kieran, and Otilio Rodriguez, O.C.D., translators.. *The Collected Works of Saint Theresa of Avila*, Volume Three. Washington, D.C.: ICS Publications, Institute of Carmelite Studies, 1985.

Keating, Thomas. *Open Mind, Open Heart: The Contemplative Dimension of the Gospel.* New York, NY: The Continuum Publishing Company, 1995.

Lieberman, David J. *Never Be Lied to Again.* New York, NY: St. Martin's Press, 1998.

Linn, S.J., Matthew and Dennis Linn. *Healing Life's Hurts.* Mahwah, NJ: Paulist Press, 1993 ed.

Lyons, Enda. *Jesus: Self-Portrait by God.* Mahwah, NJ: Paulist Press, 1994.

Mahoney, S.J., John. *The Making of Moral Theology.* New York, NY: Oxford University Press,1987.

Maloney, Newton H. *The Psychology of Religion for Ministry.* Mahwah, NJ: Paulist Press, 1995.

May, Eugene H. *Sin.* Cincinnati, OH: Pflaum/Standard, 1973.

Marmion, Abbot. *Christ in His Mysteries.* Westminster, MD: Christian Classics (Distributor, U.S.),1939.

May, Gerald G. *Addiction and Grace.* San Francisco, CA: Harper San Francisco, 1991.

McBrien, Richard P. *Catholicism.* San Francisco, CA: Harper & Row Publishers, 1981.

McCarroll, Tolbert. *Guiding God's Children.* Mahwah, NJ: Paulist Press, 1983.

McColgan, Daniel. *A Century of Charity.* Milwaukee, WI: Bruce Publishing, 1951.

McGloin, Kevin. *What Every Catholic Needs to Know About the Mass.* San Jose, CA: Resource Publications, Inc., 2001.

McKinney, Mary Benet. *Sharing Wisdom: A Process for Group Decision Making.* Allen, TX: Tabor Publishing, 1987.

Megargee, Edwin Inglee. *The California Psychological Inventory Handbook.* San Francisco, CA: Jossey-Bass, Inc., Publishers, 1972.

Merton, Thomas. *New Seeds of Contemplation.* New York, NY: New Directions Publishing Co., 1961.

Murphy-O'Connor, Jerome. *Paul the Letter Writer.* Collegeville, MN: The Liturgical Press, 1995.

National Conference of Catholic Bishops. *Hispanic Ministry: Three Major Documents.* Washington, D.C.: United States Catholic Conference, 1995.

National Conference of Catholic Bishops. *The Basic Plan for the Ongoing Formation of Priests.* Washington, D.C.: United States Catholic Conference, 2001.

O'Neil, CSsR, Kevin J., and Peter Black, CSsR. *The Essential Moral Handbook.* Liguori, MO: Liguori Publications, 2003.

Peck, M.D., M. Scott. *The Different Drum: Community Making and Peace.* New York, NY: Simon & Schuster, 1987.

Peck, M.D., M. Scott. *People of the Lie: The Hope for Healing Human Evil,* New York, NY: Simon & Schuster, 1983.

Powell, S.J., John. *Why Am I Afraid to Love?* Niles, IL: Argus Communications,1972.

Rahner, Karl. *The Need and the Blessing of Prayer.* Collegeville, MN: The Liturgical Press, 1997.

Rausch, Thomas P. *Priesthood Today: An Appraisal.* Mahwah, NJ: Paulist Press, 1992.

Robbins, Anthony. *Awaken the Giant Within: How to Take Immediate Control of Your Mental, Emotional, Physical and Financial Destiny.* New York, NY: Simon & Schuster, 1991.

Rodriguez, O.C.D., Otilio and Kieran Kavanaugh, O.C.D. *The Collected Works of Saint Teresa of Avila,* Volume Two. Washington, D.C.: ICS Publications, Institute of Carmelite Studies, 1980.

Rohr, Richard. *Contemplation in Action.* New York, NY: The Crossroad Publishing Company, 2006.

Rohr, Richard, and Joseph Martos. *The Great Themes of Scripture: New Testament.* Cincinnati, OH: St. Anthony Messenger Press, 1988.

Rolheiser, Ronald. *The Holy Longing: The Search for a Christian Spirituality.* New York, NY: Doubleday, 1999.

Sack, Steven Mitchell. *The Working Woman's Legal Survival Guide.* Paramus, NJ: Prentice Hall, 1998.

Sadler, Jeff. *The Long Term Care Handbook* (2nd ed.), Cincinnati, OH: The National Underwriter Company, 1998.

Sande, Ken. *The Peacemaker.* Grand Rapids, MI: Baker Books, 2004.

Santa, Thomas M. *Sacred Refuge: Why and How to Make a Retreat.* Notre Dame, IN: Ave Maria Press, 2005.

Senior, Donald. *The Gospel of Matthew.* Nashville, TN: Abingdon Press, 1997.

Short, Robert L. *The Gospel According to Peanuts.* Louisville, KY: Westminster John Knox Press, 1999 edition.

Stuart-Hamilton, Ian. *The Psychology of Ageing* (2nd ed.). London: Jessica Kingsley Publishers, 1994.

Temple, Gray. *52 Ways to Help Homeless People.* Nashville, TN: Thomas Nelson Publishers, 1991.

Thomas, Caroline M., *The Ministry of the Assembly.* San Jose, CA: Resource Publications, Inc., 2008.

Tierney, Mark. *Blessed Columba Marmion.* Collegeville, MN: The Liturgical Press, 2001.

Tuoti, Frank X. *Why Not Be a Mystic?* New York, NY: Crossroad Classic, 1995.

United States Catholic Conference, Inc.—Libreria Editrice Vaticana. *Catechism of the Catholic Church.* New York, NY: William H. Sadlier, Inc., 1994.

United States Catholic Conference, Inc. *General Directory for Catechesis.* Washington, D.C.: United States Catholic Conference, 1997.

United States Conference of Catholic Bishops. *Co-Workers in the Vineyard of the Lord.* Washington, D.C.: USCCB, 2005.

United States Conference of Catholic Bishops. *United States Catholic Catechism for Adults.* Washington, D.C.: USCCB, 2006.

Vogt, Susan V. *Raising Kids Who Will Make a Difference.* Chicago, IL: Loyola Press, 2002.

Weigel, George. *The Courage to Be Catholic.* New York, NY: Basic Books, 2002.

Whitehead, Evelyn Eaton; and Whitehead, James D. *Seasons of Strength.* Winona, MN: Saint Mary's Press, 1995.

Wuebker, M.D., Margherita Giuliani. *How to Cope with Growing Older.* Nashville, TN: Winston-Derek Publishers, Inc.,1988.